INSIDE THE MINDS

Electronic Records Management and e-Discovery

Leading Lawyers on Navigating Recent Trends, Understanding Rules and Regulations, and Implementing an e-Discovery Strategy

AF815400

ASPATORE

Mat #41072731

©2010 Thomson Reuters/Aspatore
All rights reserved. Printed in the United States of America.

Inside the Minds Project Manager, Caitlin Keiper; edited by Michaela Falls; proofread by Melanie Zimmerman

No part of this publication may be reproduced or distributed in any form or by any means, or stored in a database or retrieval system, except as permitted under Sections 107 or 108 of the U.S. Copyright Act, without prior written permission of the publisher. This book is printed on acid-free paper.

Material in this book is for educational purposes only. This book is sold with the understanding that neither any of the authors nor the publisher is engaged in rendering legal, accounting, investment, or any other professional service. Neither the publisher nor the authors assume any liability for any errors or omissions or for how this book or its contents are used or interpreted or for any consequences resulting directly or indirectly from the use of this book. For legal advice or any other, please consult your personal lawyer or the appropriate professional.

The views expressed by the individuals in this book (or the individuals on the cover) do not necessarily reflect the views shared by the companies they are employed by (or the companies mentioned in this book). The employment status and affiliations of authors with the companies referenced are subject to change.

Aspatore books may be purchased for educational, business, or sales promotional use. For information, please e-mail West.customer.service@thomson.com.

ISBN 978-0-314-26819-8

For corrections, updates, comments or any other inquiries please e-mail TLR.AspatoreEditorial@thomson.com.

First Printing, 2010
10 9 8 7 6 5 4 3 2 1

Praise for *Inside the Minds*

"This series provides a practical and focused discussion of the leading issues in law today." – John V. Biernacki, Partner, Jones Day

"*Inside the Minds* draws from the collective experience of the best professionals. The books are informative from an academic, and, more importantly, practical perspective. I highly recommend them." – Keith M. Aurzada, Partner, Bryan Cave LLP

"Aspatore's *Inside the Minds* series provides practical, cutting edge advice from those with insight into the real world challenges that confront businesses in the global economy." – Michael Bednarek, Partner, Shearman & Sterling LLP

"What to read when you want to be in the know—topical, current, practical, and useful information on areas of the law that everyone is talking about." – Erika L. Morabito, Partner, Patton Boggs LLP

"Some of the best insight around from sources in the know" – Donald R. Kirk, Shareholder, Fowler White Boggs PA

"The *Inside the Minds* series provides a unique window into the strategic thinking of key players in business and law." – John M. Sylvester, Partner, K&L Gates LLP

"Comprehensive analysis and strategies you won't find anywhere else." – Stephen C. Stapleton, Of Counsel, Dykema Gossett PLLC

"The *Inside the Minds* series is a real hands-on, practical resource for cutting edge issues." – Trey Monsour, Partner, Haynes and Boone LLP

"A tremendous resource, amalgamating commentary from leading professionals that is presented in a concise, easy to read format." – Alan H. Aronson, Shareholder, Akerman Senterfitt

"Unique and invaluable opportunity to gain insight into the minds of experienced professionals." – Jura C. Zibas, Partner, Lewis Brisbois Bisgaard & Smith LLP

"A refreshing collection of strategic insights, not dreary commonplaces, from some of the best of the profession." – Roger J. Magnuson, Partner, Dorsey & Whitney LLP

"Provides valuable insights by experienced practitioners into practical and theoretical developments in today's ever-changing legal world." – Elizabeth Gray, Partner, Willkie, Farr & Gallagher LLP

"This series provides invaluable insight into the practical experiences of lawyers in the trenches." – Thomas H. Christopher, Partner, Kilpatrick Stockton LLP

ASPATORE

www.Aspatore.com

Aspatore Books, a Thomson Reuters business, exclusively publishes C-Level executives (CEO, CFO, CTO, CMO, Partner) from the world's most respected companies and law firms. C-Level Business Intelligence™, as conceptualized and developed by Aspatore Books, provides professionals of all levels with proven business intelligence from industry insiders—direct and unfiltered insight from those who know it best—as opposed to third-party accounts offered by unknown authors and analysts. Aspatore Books is committed to publishing an innovative line of business and legal books, those which lay forth principles and offer insights that when employed, can have a direct financial impact on the reader's business objectives. In essence, Aspatore publishes critical tools for all business professionals.

Inside the Minds

The *Inside the Minds* series provides readers of all levels with proven legal and business intelligence from C-Level executives and lawyers (CEO, CFO, CTO, CMO, Partner) from the world's most respected companies and law firms. Each chapter is comparable to a white paper or essay and is a future-oriented look at where an industry, profession, or topic is heading and the most important issues for future success. Each author has been selected based upon their experience and C-Level standing within the professional community. *Inside the Minds* was conceived in order to give readers actual insights into the leading minds of top lawyers and business executives worldwide, presenting an unprecedented look at various industries and professions.

Contents

Developments and Trends in the World of Electronic Discovery

Catherine R. Connors and Mark E. Porada

Partners

Pierce Atwood LLP

ASPATORE

Introduction

In just a few short years since the Federal Rules of Civil Procedure were amended in December 2006 to expressly address electronic discovery, the life of litigators involved in complex litigation has changed dramatically. Because of the corporate world's shift starting in the 1990s from recording and storing everything in paper files stuffed in a file cabinet to storing things on computers, in e-mail, and on disks, the federal rules had not kept up with the times, and there was no uniform practice among the courts for dealing with discovery related to electronic forms of documents. Discovery in big cases used to involve sitting in a warehouse looking through boxes of musty paper. Now, following the 2006 rule amendments, it often involves sitting at your computer scanning through millions of pages of documents and e-mails that have been downloaded from a company's server or other electronic storage devices. The task is the same (trying to ferret out relevant information from the sea of extraneous materials), but the format has changed, and along with it the magnitude and costs involved in any high-stakes litigation. This chapter briefly explores how we got to where we are, issues to consider in the course of any lawsuit likely to involve electronic discovery, and the outlook for further changes to the e-discovery rules.

Background

The federal rules now specifically acknowledge that "electronically stored information" is subject to discovery in the normal course, FED. R. CIV. P. 34(a)(1)(A), at least unless it is "not reasonably accessible because of undue burden or cost." FED. R. CIV. P. 26(b)(2)(B). As with most things, the devil is in the details, and the focus in most e-discovery disputes is on how accessible the information is, the other party's need for it, and what the costs would be to retrieve it. Parties are supposed to try to agree on the scope of e-discovery at the onset of a lawsuit, *see* FED. R. CIV. P. 26(f), and the court's initial scheduling order should address the basic scope of electronic discovery. *See* FED. R. CIV. P. 16(b)(3). And of course, to make sure people actually follow the amended rules, there is the threat of sanctions if a party fails to produce electronic information that is requested by an opponent, unless the information is "lost as a result of the routine, good-faith operation of an electronic information system." FED. R. CIV. P. 37(f).

The rules themselves provide only half the analysis in any e-discovery dispute, with the remainder resolved on a case-by-case basis by the courts. Nevertheless, not all judges are considered equal in the field of electronic discovery, with some standing out as the trendsetters who fill in the gaps left by the rules, such as when the obligation to preserve documents arises, how to determine the scope of electronic data that must be preserved, or how to balance the costs between the parties.

Judge Shira Scheindlin of the U.S. District Court for the Southern District of New York paved the way in addressing these types of issues in a series of opinions in *Zubulake v. UBS Warburg LLC*, a case involving gender discrimination and retaliation. Judge Scheindlin's decisions provided the framework both for the development of the 2006 amendments to the federal rules, and for how courts analyze e-discovery issues as they arise today. *See* Zubulake v. UBS Warburg LLC, 217 F.R.D. 309 (S.D.N.Y. 2003) (analyzing production of e-mails from backup tapes and consideration of cost-shifting); Zubulake v. UBS Warburg LLC, 230 F.R.D. 290 (S.D.N.Y. 2003) (involving a plaintiff's ability to disclose contents of deposition of a defendant's employee concerning a company's e-mail retention policies); Zubulake v. UBS Warburg LLC, 216 F.R.D. 280 (S.D.N.Y. 2003) (addressing costs of restoring backup tapes); Zubulake v. UBS Warburg LLC, 220 F.R.D. 212 (S.D.N.Y. 2003) (awarding sanctions against a defendant for violating the duty to preserve evidence); Zubulake v. UBS Warburg LLC, 229 F.R.D. 422 (S.D.N.Y. 2004) (holding that a jury would be given an adverse inference instruction with respect to e-mails that had been destroyed by a defendant's employees in defiance of instructions by counsel not to do so).

Judge Scheindlin's most recent e-discovery decision in Pension Comm. of Univ. of Montreal Pension Plan v. Banc of Am. Securities LLC, 685 F. Supp. 2d (S.D.N.Y. 2010), subtitled "*Zubulake* Revisited: Six Years Later," provides a further attempt to delineate across-the-board standards for assessing electronic discovery compliance by both parties and outside counsel. The *Pension Committee* decision already has drawn a response from other noted e-discovery jurists, such as Judge Lee H. Rosenthal of the U.S. District Court for the Southern District of Texas and current chair of the Federal Judicial Conference Advisory Committee for the Federal Rules of Civil Procedure. *See* Rimkus v Cammarata, 688 F. Supp. 2d 598 (S.D. Tex. 2010). Parsing the judges' varying analyses is beyond the scope of this chapter; suffice it to say that any discussion about the origins and boundaries of electronic discovery would be incomplete without a reference to their opinions, which have had significant influence throughout the federal judiciary.

Many federal district courts around the country have adopted their own local rules in recent years to provide further flesh on the e-discovery parameters set forth in the federal rules. The local rules generally provide a framework and deadlines by which parties and their lawyers have to consult and attempt to achieve consensus concerning the scope and extent of electronic discovery to be pursued in each case. The district court in Maryland, in particular, promulgated an early set of protocols that have been followed by other districts around the country interested in providing some measure of consistency in how electronic discovery is approached from one case to the next and among the judges on each court. More recently, the Seventh Circuit Court of Appeals adopted a set of principles and a standing order for the handling of e-discovery within its district courts.

As with many technology-related issues, the state courts by and large have been slower than the federal courts in delving into e-discovery, although quite a few states have adopted amendments to their own state rules of civil procedure that track the 2006 amendments to the federal rules. Maine, for instance, amended its rules effective August 2008, mostly tracking the federal electronic discovery rules, with two significant exceptions. First, Maine Rule 26 was amended to provide that, if electronic discovery would be unduly burdensome but nevertheless is deemed necessary, the court "shall impose on the requesting party the reasonable expense of producing such electronically stored information." ME. R. CIV. P. 26(b)(6). That mandated cost shifting differs from the federal rule, which provides only that in such circumstances the court "may specify conditions for the discovery," which could include cost-shifting to the requesting party. FED. R. CIV. P. 26(b)(2)(B).

Second, the Maine advisory committee notes appear to back away from the idea that some form of electronic discovery may be appropriate in every case, stating that the fact "that the discovery rules provide for the production of such information does not suggest that discovery of electronically stored information is appropriate in every case." ME. R. CIV. P. 16 adv. comm. notes (July 2008). Those distinctions highlight the reluctance on the part of many state courts to fully embrace the full scope of electronic discovery contemplated by the federal rules, along with the inherent conflicts and time-consuming discovery disputes that go along with them.

As a practical matter, the decision whether to file a lawsuit in federal or state court often has a significant impact on the scope—if any—of electronic discovery that will occur in a particular case. There are always exceptions, and a complex commercial dispute between two sophisticated companies likely will involve some measure of e-discovery regardless of where the complaint was filed, as both sides will want it. But in smaller cases or cases involving a lone plaintiff suing a corporate defendant, the decision to file the case in state court often signals a diminished interest on the part of the plaintiff in aggressively pursuing costly and voluminous electronic discovery from the defendant. As a result, despite having rules that may mirror the federal rules, state courts on the whole are not being exposed to e-discovery disputes on anywhere near the same scale as the federal courts. That means that when e-discovery disputes do arise in state court, they are likely to raise novel issues for the particular judge involved, and there may be less of a track record for predicting the outcome.

Issues to Consider When Electronic Discovery Is Involved

The issues that drive most considerations regarding electronic discovery are cost and burden. In today's society, the quantity of electronic records created and retained by individuals in their personal lives is incredible, and the amount generated by businesses is even more staggering. While in the old days a large case might involve a warehouse full of boxes of old documents, in today's litigation there can be enough data that, if printed out, would fill entire football stadiums to the roof. As a practical matter, there is no way to review and process all of the data, and the vast majority of it is irrelevant to the issues in dispute in any particular case. Trying to find ways to cull through the mountains of information to (i) determine what you have, and (ii) separate out the important information from the extraneous, is always the challenge.

In litigation where electronic discovery is a significant focus of the overall discovery effort, the e-discovery component often dwarfs the other "traditional" forms of discovery also being conducted in the case (e.g., hard paper discovery, written interrogatories, depositions, etc.) in terms of expense and effort involved. Many judges and lawyers who have not had extensive exposure to e-discovery tend to simplify matters and assume that gathering and producing responsive data is as simple as pushing the proverbial button on a computer. Unfortunately, the process needed to gather and review electronic data is never that easy, either to perform or even to explain in response to a motion to compel or other attack by the opposing party. In cases where there is an allegation that trade secrets have been misappropriated and may exist on someone else's computer or server, just hiring a forensic expert to mirror image the hard drive or server and perform a basic analysis can cost up to $10,000 or more, depending on the complexity of the data. In cases where production of electronic mail is an issue (and it almost always will be in any case where e-discovery is on the horizon, since most people communicate by e-mail now in their business lives rather than by any "old-fashioned" means like talking on the phone or in person), the sky is the limit. As a result, concerns over the burdens of responding to electronic discovery can drive the direction of litigation and essentially force settlement in certain cases where a party concludes that it simply is not worth the effort to defend a case, incurring all of the discovery related costs along the way, where the ultimate outcome is uncertain.

Because of the impacts e-discovery can have on the course of litigation, it is important to consider how best to handle electronic aspects of the discovery process as early on in the litigation as possible. The local rules adopted by some federal district courts, which set up specific deadlines and time frames that require opposing counsel to discuss these issues, are a good start. But nothing can be resolved without early and comprehensive discussions between counsel and appropriate information technology staff on the client's end to gain an understanding of what type of electronic data is available, how it can be accessed and searched, and what exactly is involved in doing so. After gaining a basic understanding of one's own client's information technology, contacting opposing counsel to attempt to agree on a framework for pursuing any electronic discovery makes sense for everyone involved. Although most negotiated protocols for handing e-discovery are likely to benefit one side or the other at various points in the process, at the end of the day those momentary blips tend to even out, in all but the rarest of cases, with a smoother and balanced approach for all of the parties.

One issue in particular about which opposing counsel should attempt to reach agreement involves the process for compiling responsive e-mail. Rational lawyers should realize that demanding that the opposing party search through every one of its e-mails for all 5,000 of its employees over a period of ten years is not going to lead to anything productive. The opposing counsel will never agree to it, and more importantly, the court will never require it. Forcing the judge to involve him or herself and rule on ridiculous positions never gains any favor with the court, and only sours further dealings with opposing counsel. There are a number of ways to approach e-mail productions. As counsel for the party that will be searching for and producing e-mails, one could wait for the other side to propose particular custodians whose e-mail should be searched, along with search terms to use in the process. In some cases that may make sense, to avoid educating the other side unnecessarily and perhaps pointing them to sources of data they had not themselves thought to seek. In many other cases, however, the better approach may be for the party that is going to have to produce the e-mails to take the initiative. For example, be the first to send opposing counsel a list of the twenty custodians you think are most likely to have relevant and responsive e-mail, and explain why. Propose the handful of key search terms that you think are likely to capture the bulk of whatever responsive e-mail is out there. Taking the lead on explaining what you propose to do, and then offering the other side the chance to respond with any additional reasonable suggestions of its own, helps keep your client in control of the work it is going to have to do, and in the event an agreement cannot be worked out between the parties and you have to resort to the court for guidance, the efforts go a long way toward establishing the good faith and reasonableness of your approach. *See, e.g.*, Surplus Source Group LLC v. Mid Am. Engine Inc., 2009 WL 961207 (E.D. Tex. Apr. 8, 2009) (rewarding a defendant in a discovery dispute where the defendant had "shown a persistent willingness to aide the Plaintiffs in crafting an ESI search that would yield the documents if they do, in fact, exist"); William A. Gross Constr. Assocs. Inc. v. Am. Mfg. Mut. Ins. Co256 F.R.D. 134 (S.D.N.Y. 2009) (issuing "a wake-up call to the Bar in this District about the need for careful thought, quality control, testing, and cooperation with opposing counsel in designing search terms or 'keywords' to be used to produce e-mails or other electronically stored information"); Lapin v. Goldman, Sachs & Co., 2009 WL 222788 (S.D.N.Y. Jan. 23, 2009) (requiring collaborative effort between parties to devise appropriate e-mail search parameters). There has never been a reported decision where one side proposed even semi-reasonable e-discovery search parameters and the other side simply refused to do anything, where the latter side prevailed. Appearances do make a difference, and having the appearance right from the start of one willing to negotiate and work toward reasonable solutions can be the tie breaker when courts reluctantly get involved in these types of disputes.

Likewise, where there are disputes about the contents of computer drives that will require forensic examination, it is a good idea to start that process as early as possible in the litigation. Inevitably there will be disputes between the parties over whether to allow one side to access the other's proprietary data at all, or over the scope of that access even where there is general agreement that an inspection can take place. Those disputes may need to be resolved by the court, which can take weeks or months, depending on the pace of the court's docket. Once the scope of the inspection is finalized, there is usually a significant amount of coordination that has to occur between the independent computer forensic expert and in-house IT staff from at least one of the parties, to make sure that the expert knows what to look for, how it will be accessed and preserved, and the format for reporting the inspection results. All of that takes time (and money) to complete, so this process should be commenced quickly after the outset of the lawsuit.

One of the most important considerations in any electronic discovery project involves the measures taken to preserve the attorney-client privilege and work product doctrine. With any large-scale e-discovery production, which may involve hundreds of thousands or even millions of pages of data, it is almost impossible to prevent the inadvertent disclosure of some number of arguably protected documents. A page-by-page review of all of the data before it is produced may be the most thorough method for avoiding inadvertent disclosure, but may not be practical or even required, given the volume of a particular production. In addition, even the most foolproof method usually has some flaws; after all, it is called "inadvertent" disclosure for a reason. The solution, contemplated in part by the federal rules amendments, *see* FED. R. CIV. P. 26(b)(5)(B), often is to enter into a stipulated protective order and agreement between the parties at the beginning of discovery to address these concerns. Unless the discovery is anticipated to be almost entirely one-sided, with one party having very little to produce but the other having truckloads of relevant information, it benefits both sides to work out an arrangement in advance. Agreements usually involve some form of "clawback" arrangement, in which a party that discovers that it has inadvertently produced an arguably protected document may simply notify the other side and demand the document's return or destruction. Typically, the receiving party is obliged to return the document, subject to the right to challenge the document's privileged status if there are appropriate grounds for doing so, independent of the inadvertent production itself.

Concluding Thoughts

Someone who is reading the case law that comes out each week involving electronic discovery disputes may get a jaundiced view of what is actually taking place. The vast majority of the reported decisions involve egregious sets of facts, with parties or their lawyers willfully concealing or destroying documents, flagrantly disobeying court orders to produce materials, or actively turning a blind eye to troves of electronic data that everyone agrees is responsive to outstanding discovery requests. Many of those cases are discussed on www.maineevidence.com, the e-discovery blog we maintain that analyzes developments and best practices for electronic discovery. In those types of cases, the courts are not hesitant to impose serious sanctions, ranging from payment of thousands (or even millions) of dollars in opposing counsel's fees, to the adoption of adverse inference instructions that will be given to the jury that essentially tell the jury to assume that there was bad evidence in the documents that were never produced, to the ultimate sanction of dismissal for malfeasant plaintiffs or default judgment for non-complying defendants. Reading only those reported cases could give the impression that there is a lot of discovery abuse occurring, and that courts are indiscriminately imposing crushing sanctions.

The real story is likely not so dramatic. As with many areas of the law, and particularly in the arena of discovery disputes, the cases with the juiciest facts or the ones in which the judge wants to set an example to discourage similar behavior are the ones that tend to get resolved by written, publishable decisions. Cases involving minor disputes or alleged infractions resulting in no sanctions get resolved with oral rulings or margin orders that never see the light of day, outside the context of the specific case in which they were entered. In reality, in most cases, the rule of reason applies with respect to electronic discovery, just as it always has with any other form of discovery. If what a party seeks appears to be reasonable to the court, it will be required. If the costs or difficulties in pulling together the responsive information greatly outweigh the likely value of what is sought, the court will conclude that the discovery is unreasonable.

All that really has changed with the advent of electronic discovery is the magnitude of data to be mined, the means of doing so, and the relative scale of costs involved. Although the spectrum of burdens a party is expected to undertake in a typical case has shifted to accommodate the difficulties associated with electronic data, there still is a range of reasonableness to which a party can expect to be held.

Because the costs and expectations associated with electronic discovery have become the predominant cost in many lawsuits, a number of organizations have issued reports in recent months that address the concern that some parties are using the electronic discovery process as an end in itself, rather than a means toward an end. The Defense Research Institute (DRI) issued a report in January 2009, and the American College of Trial Lawyers and the Institute for the Advancement of the American Legal System issued a joint report in March 2009. Almost universally, those reports, among others, recommend a revamping of the role of discovery in the American civil justice system, with a particular emphasis on reining in the scope of e-discovery in particular.

Essentially what the commentators have suggested is a restructuring of the discovery rules to provide a more individualized tailoring of the scope and type of discovery to the specifics of each case. While extensive electronic discovery may make sense in a complicated intellectual property dispute between ABC Corp. and XYC Inc., it probably makes less sense in a dispute between a consumer and a local business. The federal rules already implicitly recognize those distinctions, but the importance of proportionality between the scope of the case and the scope of discovery could be better articulated. Too often, those considerations are not given the proper attention until too late in the process, or after substantial costs already have been incurred, sometimes with little relevant information gained in spite of the massive scope of data produced. If nothing else, the proposals advanced by these groups are sure to lead to a lively debate among lawyers and interest groups. One thing is certain—the pace of technology is not slowing down, and so the electronic discovery issues of the next decade are sure to raise a host of new complications that have yet to be seen.

Key Takeaways

- Because of the impacts e-discovery can have on the course of litigation, it is important to consider how best to handle electronic aspects of the discovery process as early on in the litigation as possible. Nothing can be resolved without early and comprehensive discussions between counsel and appropriate information technology staff on the client's end to gain an understanding of what type of electronic data is available, how it can be accessed and searched, and what exactly is involved in doing so.
- After gaining a basic understanding of one's own client's information technology, contacting opposing counsel to attempt to agree on a framework for pursuing any electronic discovery makes sense for everyone involved.
- The party that is going to have to produce the e-mails should take the initiative. Be the first to send opposing counsel a list of the twenty custodians you think are most likely to have relevant and responsive e-mail, and explain why. Propose the handful of key search terms that you think are likely to capture the bulk of whatever responsive e-mail is out there.
- Unless discovery is anticipated to be almost entirely one-sided, it benefits both sides to work out an arrangement in advance, such as some form of "clawback" arrangement, in which a party that discovers that it has inadvertently produced an arguably protected document may simply notify the other side and demand the document's return or destruction.

Related Resources

1. Seventh Circuit Electronic Discovery Pilot Program (Phase I), *available at* www.ilcd.uscourts.gov/Statement%20-%20Phase%20One.pdf
2. Suggested Protocol for Discovery of Electronically Stored Information ("ESI") (D. Md.), *available at* www.mdd.uscourts.gov/news/news/ESIProtocol.pdf

***Catherine R. Connors**, a partner at Pierce Atwood LLP, practices primarily in the area of appellate litigation—both civil and criminal—in the federal and state courts, including petitions for review of administrative decisions. She has argued more than one hundred appeals, primarily in the United States Courts of Appeals and the Maine Supreme Judicial Court. Ms. Connors received her Bachelor's degree magna cum laude from Northwestern University (Phi Beta Kappa; 1981), and her J.D. cum laude from Northwestern University School of Law (Order of the Coif 1984), where she served on the editorial board of the* Northwestern University Law Review. *After law school, she served as a law clerk for then Chief Judge John F. Grady of the U.S. District Court, Northern District of Illinois. She joined Pierce Atwood in 1986.*

***Mark E. Porada**, a partner at Pierce Atwood LLP, has a broad litigation practice that draws upon his experience in all phases of state and federal litigation. Mr. Porada has successfully represented both national corporations and smaller companies in a wide range of disputes involving complex litigation, commercial disputes, insurance coverage disputes, and ERISA litigation in the state and federal courts throughout Maine, Massachusetts, New Hampshire, and California. In recent years, Mr. Porada has acted as trial counsel in jury trials in federal courts in Maine and Massachusetts, and has argued before the U.S. Court of Appeals for the First Circuit. Mr. Porada also has broad experience handling electronic discovery in complex cases. Among other matters, in recent years Mr. Porada was responsible for overseeing a two-year long discovery process in a case pending in federal court in Massachusetts that involved the production of millions of pages of documents and electronic records.*

Mr. Porada received his B.A. from Trinity College, Phi Beta Kappa, (1994), and J.D., summa cum laude, from the University of Pennsylvania Law School (Order of the Coif, 1997), where he was a senior editor of the University of Pennsylvania Law Review *and served as a member of the Moot Court Board. Mr. Porada served as a law clerk to Judge Norma Shapiro for the U.S. District Court, Eastern District of Pennsylvania, after graduating from law school.*

Taking a Proactive Stance in the e-Discovery Process

Joseph A. DiMenno

Shareholder

Dickie, McCamey & Chilcote PC

ASPATORE

Recent Trends in e-Discovery

Generally, the rules of discovery for electronic records and e-discovery are the same, with both following the previously established rules of civil procedure for either the state or federal courts. However, given the unique nature of electronically stored information (hereinafter ESI) and how it is quickly becoming the major form of evidence in most civil matters, the rules of civil procedure for the federal courts have seen the need to address ESI and its management in the litigation process. At this time, most state courts tend to follow the lead established by the federal courts of their jurisdiction; however, some states, such as Ohio, have addressed ESI through their own state court rules of civil procedure.

Factors that are driving the need for additional regulation in this area include the need for consistency and predictability. Having such guideposts will offer structure and efficiency for the parties, their counsel, and the courts. The primary mover or catalyst for change in this area has been the Sedona Conference, but other organizations such as state and local bar associations along with the courts themselves, through rules advisory committees, have contributed to recent changes.

The Sedona Conference is a charitable organization based in Arizona dedicated to the advancement of law in a variety of specialties. With regard to e-discovery, the organization came to the forefront when it created Working Group 1 (WG1) in the spring of 2002. Nearly a year later in March 2003, WG1 issued a public comment version of The Sedona Principles addressing electronic document production. These principles have been subsequently cited for guidance by the federal courts and federal rules advisory committees on how best to adapt to the existence of electronically stored information and its treatment in litigation.

Given the large volume of data often associated with ESI, parties have sought ways to fulfill their production obligations while controlling costs. With any large data set, there is always the fear of inadvertent productions. As a result, parties often agree to disclosure waivers anticipating such an incident. Two common disclosure waivers include "quick peek" agreements or "clawback" agreements between the parties often memorialized by court order to set parameters on waiver.

"Quick peek" agreements facilitate discovery by allowing the requesting party to take a "quick peek" at ESI without the producing party undertaking the time and expense in previewing the entire population of ESI to eliminate non-responsive and privileged information. Then, during the course of its "quick peek," the requesting party identifies which ESI records it wants formally produced. In essence, this shifts the burden of initial review upon the requesting party, but at the risk of sharing information with the requesting party that might be later withheld when the producing party only produces those documents that are responsive and not privileged. The compromise for such a full disclosure is that the requesting party agrees that it will return, not use, and not claim waiver with respect to any non-responsive or privileged information that it saw during the quick peek.

Most parties hesitate to permit such an unfettered release of documents without review, fearing that third parties might claim that such agreements of non-waiver do not bind them. Further, most parties never want the opposing side to ever see such material in the first place and have a fundamental issue with the concept of a production of documents with little or no review. An option that allows for more flexibility with large sets of data subject to production is a clawback agreement, compelling the return of inadvertently produced protected materials without a fear of waiver of any privilege protecting the document.

The issue of inadvertent waiver of attorney-client privilege or work-product privilege is a matter best addressed as early as the first scheduling conference with the court. The responsibility for enforcing the e-discovery rules initially belongs to the parties themselves, but ultimately the court shall rule on such disputes.

These practices highlight the need for early assessment of what efforts will be required to retrieve and protect relevant ESI, since the answers to these early questions affect both timelines for case management orders as well as costs for discovery obligations.

Legal Standards for e-Discovery: Relevant Cases

Significant cases that have tested the legal standards for e-discovery include the Zubulake series of cases from Judge Scheindlin of the federal district court for the Southern District of New York. These cases tested the legal standards of the duties of preservation and cost-shifting relating to e-discovery requests. As Judge Scheindlin opined:

> [T]he universe of discoverable material has expanded exponentially. The more information there is to discover, the more expensive it is to discover all the relevant information until, in the end, "discovery is not just about uncovering the truth, but also about how much of the truth parties can afford to disinter."

Zubulake v. UBS Warburg (Zubulake I), 217 F.R.D. 309, 311 (S.D.N.Y. 2003) (quoting Rowe Entm't Inc. v. William Morris Agency Inc., 205 F.R.D. 421, 423 (S.D.N.Y. 2002).

In the line of cases factually, Zubulake was a securities trader specializing in Asian securities. She filed suit under federal, state, and city law against UBS, her former employer, alleging gender discrimination, failure to promote, and retaliation. She estimated that she might have been entitled to as much as $13 million in damages for full back and front pay related to her claims, not including attorney's fees and punitive damages. She also claimed that key evidence was located in various e-mails exchanged between UBS employees that now exist on backup tapes. UBS contended that restoring those e-mails would be costly. Zubulake moved for an order to compel UBS to produce the e-mails at its own expense and an order permitting her to release the transcript of the deposition of the manager of Global Messaging to securities regulators. *Zubulake I*, 217 F.R.D. at 311-13.

Zubulake I: Zubulake v. UBS Warburg, 217 F.R.D. 309 (S.D.N.Y. May 13, 2003)

The issue was to what extent is inaccessible electronic data discoverable, and who should pay for its production. The court held that Zubulake was entitled to discovery of the requested e-mails as long as they were related to her claims. Since UBS recognized that Zubulake was entitled to discovery, it tried to urge the court to shift the cost of production to Zubulake. *Zubulake I*, 217 F.R.D. at 316-17.

The court determined that cost-shifting of document production should only be considered when electronic discovery imposes an undue burden or expense on the responding party. A determination of undue burden depends on whether the evidence is kept in an accessible or inaccessible format. *Id.* at 317-320. The court modified the *Rowe* factors, Rowe Entm't Inc. v. William Morris Agency Inc., 205 F.R.D. 421, 429-32 (S.D.N.Y. 2002), and defined seven factors for determining when shifting costs of document production to the requesting party is appropriate, weighted more or less in the following order:

1. The extent to which the request is specifically tailored to discover relevant information
2. The availability of such information from other sources
3. The total cost of production, compared to the amount in controversy
4. The total cost of production, compared to the resources available to each party
5. The relative ability of each party to control costs and its incentive to do so
6. The importance of the issues at stake in the litigation
7. The relative benefits to the parties obtaining the information *Zubulake I*, 217 F.R.D. at 320-24.

Accordingly, UBS was ordered to produce, at its expense, the requested responsive e-mails from five backup tapes selected by Zubulake as well as an affidavit detailing its search. After those steps were completed, the Court would conduct the appropriate cost-shifting analysis. *Id.* at 324.

Zubulake II: Zubulake v. UBS Warburg, 230 F.R.D. 290 (S.D.N.Y. May 13, 2003)

UBS produced Christopher Behny, manager of Global Messaging, for deposition. He testified to the structure of UBS's backup system and backup tape destruction/retention policy. Zubulake v. UBS Warburg (Zubulake II), 230 F.R.D. 290, 291 (S.D.N.Y. 2003).

This case addresses the issue of whether Zubulake was allowed to disclose the Behny deposition to the NYSE and NASD to discharge her ethical duties when UBS designated such information as confidential. Release of information concerning UBS's technological capabilities and practices would create a competitive disadvantage for the firm. Therefore, the court ruled that since Zubulake was not a member of either the NYSE or NASD, they only viewed her request as an attempt to gain leverage against UBS in her suit. Since the reporting regulations she relied on did not apply to her, her motion was denied. *Id.* at 292-93.

Zubulake III: Zubulake v. UBS Warburg, 216 F.R.D. 280 (S.D.N.Y. July 24, 2003)

After reviewing the results of the sample restoration of certain e-mails on a small group of backup tapes, Zubulake moved for an order to compel UBS to produce all remaining backup e-mails at its expense. UBS argued that the costs should be shifted to Zubulake. Zubulake v. UBS Warburg (Zubulake III), 216 F.R.D. 280, 282-83 (S.D.N.Y. 2003).

Using the cost-shifting factors, the court ordered Zubulake to share in the costs of restoration, but held that UBS must bear the majority of costs. The court also ordered UBS to bear all of the costs once documents were restored from an inaccessible format to an accessible format to review the restored documents for privilege. *Id.* at 285-291. The court determined that the general rules of discovery applied once data was accessible for two reasons. First, the producing party always has the exclusive ability to control costs of review. Second, the reviewing party unilaterally decides on the review protocol. *Id.*

Zubulake IV: Zubulake v. UBS Warburg, 220 F.R.D. 212 (S.D.N.Y. Oct. 22, 2003)

This case detailed the scope of a litigant's duty to preserve electronic documents and the consequences of a failure to preserve documents that fall within the scope of that duty. During the restoration process mandated in *Zubulake II*, certain backup tapes were missing and certain e-mails relevant to the employment discrimination were not saved at all. Outside counsel for UBS orally instructed the firm to stop recycling backup tapes. Zubulake sought spoliation sanctions. Zubulake v. UBS Warburg (Zubulake IV), 220 F.R.D. 212, 215-16 (S.D.N.Y. 2003).

The court held that a party has the duty to preserve evidence when it is put on notice that the evidence is relevant to litigation or should have known the evidence may be relevant in future litigation. The scope of the duty to preserve electronic data applies only when a party reasonably anticipates litigation. The same duty to preserve also extends to key players and other employees likely to have relevant information. *Id.* at 216-19.

As a general rule, once a party reasonably anticipates litigation, it must suspend its routine document retention or destruction policy and put in place a "litigation hold" to ensure the preservation of relevant documents. A litigation hold does not apply to inaccessible backup tapes, which may continue to be recycled on the schedule set forth in the company's policy. On the other hand, if backup tapes are accessible, then such tapes would likely be subject to the litigation hold. *Id.* at 218.

An exception applies if the company can identify employee documents that are stored on backup tapes. If that is the case, the tapes should be preserved if the information contained on those tapes is not otherwise available. *Id.*

Therefore, the court determined that UBS breached its duty to preserve the backup tapes at issue and must bear Zubulake's costs for re-deposing certain witnesses due to the destruction of evidence. *Id.* at 222.

Zubulake V: Zubulake v. UBS Warburg, 229 F.R.D. 422 (S.D.N.Y. July 20, 2004)

The court reviewed information brought to light as a result of re-depositions from *Zubulake IV* and concluded that UBS willfully failed to preserve responsive e-mails. Zubulake v. UBS Warburg (Zubulake V), 229 F.R.D. 422, 439-40 (S.D.N.Y. 2004).

This case addresses counsel's obligation to ensure that relevant information is preserved. *Id.* at 432. First, counsel must issue a "litigation hold" whenever litigation is reasonably anticipated. Counsel has a duty to remind employees that the litigation hold is still in effect. *Id.* at 433. Second, counsel must communicate with "key players" and remind them of the duty to preserve. Further, counsel must become fully familiar with his client's document retention policies. Last, counsel must instruct his clients to produce all relevant data and ensure the evidence is stored in a safe place to avoid intentional or inadvertent destruction of potentially relevant data. Once counsel takes these steps, the client is fully on notice of its discovery obligations. *Id.* at 433-34.

Thus, the court ordered sanctions requiring UBS to pay costs associated with discovery and held that counsel for UBS was not blameless. *Id.* at 439-40.

Zubulake VI: Zubulake v. UBS Warburg, 231 F.R.D. 159 (S.D.N.Y. Feb. 2, 2005)

Discovery in this case closed in 2004. Zubulake v. UBS Warburg (Zubulake VI), 231 F.R.D. 159, 159 (S.D.N.Y. 2005). Defendants now seek to add after-acquired evidence as an affirmative defense. UBS alleged that the plaintiff misrepresented her reasons for termination from a previous employer on her application and claimed it would have terminated Zubulake immediately if it had known about the misrepresentations. *Id.* at 160. The court denied the defendant's motion because of a twenty-two month delay in asserting the defense, the undue prejudice it would have caused the plaintiff by necessitating a reopening of discovery, and the resulting postponement of the trial date. *Id.* at 161-63.

Zubulake VII: Zubulake v. UBS Warburg, 382 F. Supp. 2d 536 (S.D.N.Y. Mar. 16, 2005)

The plaintiff filed a motion in limine to preclude defendants from using evidence about her employment history to show her propensity for certain performance deficiencies. The court determined that the plaintiff's employment history was not admissible as habit evidence because it would cause jury confusion and undue delay in the trial proceedings. Zubulake v. UBS Warburg (Zubulake VII), 382 F. Supp. 2d 536, 540-43 (S.D.N.Y. 2005).

The defendants also filed a motion in limine to preclude alleged acts of discrimination against another UBS employee. The court allowed plaintiff to introduce this evidence because the discrimination was in relation to her gender discrimination claim. However, she could not introduce evidence pertaining to correspondence by UBS counsel on discovery matters unless the defendants opened the door. *Id.* at 544-46.

In addition, plaintiff was precluded from calling defendants' attorneys as witnesses regarding the preservation of e-mails and backup tapes because such testimony would be cumulative considering that the documents had already been produced. *Id.* at 548-49.

Components of an e-Discovery Strategy

In developing an effective e-discovery strategy for a client, you should:

1. Identify the evidence you seek from all other parties.
2. Identify the evidence you will seek to produce to support your position and identify the evidence that the other parties will seek from you to support their claims.
3. Determine the nature and identity of the sources possessing the needed evidence. These individuals are often referred to as "key players." (The level of attention given to the data obtained from the CEO of the company prior to production versus the attention given to data received from an entry level employee will vary tremendously because of the heightened sensitivity of information at the executive level. The guiding principle must always be to produce only what is relevant and non-privileged. Be mindful of efforts by the opposing party to conducting "fishing expeditions").
4. Determine the format of the ESI and its accessibility. This is important because it will most directly affect the cost of production. If an early evaluation reveals that the nature of the format is unique and not widely used and its accessibility will prove to be unduly burdensome to the producing party, the producing party may petition the court for a sharing or shifting of costs with the requesting party.
5. Ensure the preservation of the ESI. This is best done by issuing a "litigation hold" letter announcing the need to preserve all relevant data. Recent case opinions now indicate a requirement for some type of follow-up with key players, possibly through a meeting or detailed written instructions.
6. For ongoing matters, establish a protocol for collecting future ESI. If the matter at issue is ongoing, establish a system whereby all relevant data is being captured and preserved as it is being created. For example, "key players" typically create folders within their computers to hold communications related to the litigation and then periodically provide the same to counsel.

These components are generally developed through early meetings and assessments with your client. It is highly beneficial to involve the client's information technology (IT) person to understand the client's computer architecture and storage locations (as well as retention policies).

With respect to e-discovery, you have a duty to preserve evidence, and the failure to do so may cause the imposition of sanctions. Such sanctions may include, under the Federal Rules of Civil Procedure, reasonable attorney fees for failure to comply with discovery obligations and court orders. FED. R. CIV. P. 37(a).

Aside from rule-based authority, all federal courts have the inherent ability to prevent abuses of the judicial process. *See* Chambers v. Nasco Inc., 501 U.S. 32, 44-46 (1991). The court has broad powers, confined only to the sound discretion of the trial judge, to sanction parties for spoliation of evidence. Zubulake v. UBS Warburg, 229 F.R.D. 422, 430 (S.D.N.Y. 2004). Courts may apply an adverse inference that the spoiled evidence was unfavorable to the party at fault for spoliation. Swofford v. Eslinger, 671 F. Supp. 2d 1274, 1285 (M.D. Fla. 2009). The court may also impose monetary sanctions equivalent to costs incurred by the requesting party for the relevant data. *Id.* at 1287. Also, sanctions may include preclusion of evidence, due to it either being withheld or produced in an untimely manner. Unigard Sec. Ins. Co. v. Lakewood Eng'g & Mfg. Corp., 982 F.2d 363 (9th Cir. 1992).

Early assessment allows you to evaluate the strengths and weaknesses of your claims/defenses, and it provides notice of not easily accessible ESI and the likelihood of significant costs for retrieval.

An e-discovery assessment can provide critical guidance as to what is needed and what is appropriate. E-discovery can quickly become very costly; therefore, having an early understanding of the scope of ESI relative to the amount in controversy allows for a more informed management of your case, both for you as counsel and for your client. Most courts are receptive to the argument of proportionality. For example, if the amount in controversy is $300,000, the court should be more mindful of limiting discovery to readily accessible data and shifting of cost upon the requesting party if the demands become disproportional to the claims.

E-discovery becomes especially critical to the case being litigated if the communications between the parties relating to critical elements of the case primarily occur via e-mail. It can unnecessarily become a distraction to your case if faced with allegations of failing to properly undertake the necessary preservation efforts at the onset.

Attorney-Client Privilege

Depending upon the nature of the dispute, communications may exist with in-house counsel or other counsel that require the protection of the attorney-client privilege. Efforts must be undertaken to identify those attorneys who may have interacted with "key players" so that those communications may be tagged as privileged and not subject to production. One common practice is to obtain the names and e-mail addresses of all legal counsel who may have interacted with the "key players." Since many individuals have more than one e-mail address, be certain to request all e-mail addresses that may have been used for the communications. Then, through the assistance of a variety of software programs, those potentially privileged communications may be culled from the collection set and evaluated further.

Integrating the e-Discovery Process into the Litigation Strategy

Typically, the e-discovery process is integrated into the litigation strategy based on the agenda established with the client at the initial meeting relating to preservation and accessibility of key information.

Again, this step is critical to insure proper budgeting of costs, time, and effort needed to comply with the rules of civil procedure. All too often, counsel will commit to certain discovery deadlines before evaluating the quantity and accessibility of ESI. This causes delays in production schedules and possible failed compliance with court-mandated case management orders.

In the litigation process, the topic of e-discovery typically does not arise until discovery. Then, it is typically your opponent placing the most emphasis on the process. However, most federal courts now require that it be discussed at the Rule 26(f) conference. In the federal court system, the Rule 26(f) conference is a meeting with a representative of the court (typically, the judge assigned to the case) following a "Meet & Confer" between the parties. The main purpose is to set in place a discovery plan with a corresponding scheduling order or case management order. Many federal district courts now require counsel for the parties to submit a written report outlining the proposed discovery plan and specifically addressing how ESI will be handled. The federal district court for the Western District of Pennsylvania has done so and a copy of the form to be used is provided.

Implementing an e-Discovery Strategy: Key Steps

The first step in implementing an e-discovery strategy is a personal meeting with the client, and if possible, all "key players." "Key players" often include the individuals with personal knowledge about the underlying facts involved in the litigation. With the increasing role being played by ESI, an IT person should often be included in these initial discussions. Again, it is extremely beneficial to meet with the IT staff of corporate clients to learn more about storage locations of ESI and retention policies. It is important to define the scope of potential ESI at each source, as well as the storage location.

Challenges to overcome in this process include lack of cooperation from the client; lack of IT knowledge or sophistication by the client with respect to e-discovery matters; and/or the client utilizes an antiquated computer system or possibly stores its data off-site or under the management of a third party.

Technology plays a very large role in the e-discovery process, and it is becoming larger. The sooner that you can use technology in the e-discovery process the better, but you must understand what is available and how to implement it. For example, software and specialized programs exist today that allow counsel to search the data of their client before commencing extensive discovery to determine the strength and accuracy of their position. Early involvement of electronic forensics can be very valuable, especially with preservation efforts. One of the best ways to discharge the duty of preservation is to secure "clones" of all potentially relevant sources of ESI. This is best handled by a computer forensic analyst who possesses the necessary training to perform the task and the ability to certify his or her efforts.

Protecting Electronic Information during Litigation

In order to protect electronic information during litigation, it is important to immediately suspend automatic archiving or deletion activity. You should immediately image or clone all hard drivers or servers at the onset, and establish preservation rules going forward if needed for newly created ESI in order to uphold the duty to preserve. If backup tapes are involved and taken out of circulation to ensure preservation, a chain of custody log should be created so the storage of the tapes is recorded. Of course, the process is often started with the service of "litigation hold" letters upon "key players."

Implementing such a process assures counsel that all reasonable steps have been taken to preserve evidence, and avoids a sanction for failure to preserve, as well as a distraction from key issues in the case while trying to defend preservation efforts.

Types of Electronic Management Systems

Most companies utilize Microsoft Outlook for the management of e-mail, which is often important in an e-discovery effort. However, new software is also being developed, such as Clearwell, which allows for a rapid and targeted review of large amounts of e-mail, which can help tremendously with case assessment (it can even be used at the onset to review one's own data).

Some systems are easier to navigate and search than others. This, of course, affects cost. One of the most difficult electronics management systems to access for e-discovery is Lotus Notes. Lotus Notes follows a very different platform, making it difficult to review individual e-mails and attachments. Most search software is not equipped to review Lotus Notes. In addition, accessing attachments in a Lotus Notes environment can be particularly challenging. Options exist to overcome these obstacles, but they can be cost prohibitive and time consuming. Knowing if your client utilizes such a system up front is critical for determining anticipated timelines for production and if cost shifting upon the requesting party is warranted.

Helpful Resources: The Role of Experts

In order to ensure understanding of the client's electronic records management system, it is important to conduct early meetings with IT personnel. If possible, counsel should have someone with IT experience available to help ask germane follow-up questions. Informed and experienced IT personnel with an understanding about litigation are among the most helpful resources in this process.

Also helpful in the e-discovery process are computer forensic consultants. At the beginning, experts should be used for the evaluation of storage systems; later on, they can assist with preservation efforts. Experts can be very helpful for retrieval and for culling of information to prepare for review by counsel. Further, the use of experts can be cited by counsel as an example of how serious preservation efforts were taken by a party.

e-Discovery Requests

The most common e-discovery request in litigation is that ESI be produced in native format, meaning that it will have the corresponding metadata available. Metadata is information that accompanies an electronic document or communication but often remains unseen or hidden. Metadata may provide information about the means of creation, the purpose of the data, the time and date of creation, the creator or author of data, and location of the data on a network where the data was created. This metadata can be particularly useful to the receiving party, since much of the metadata can be used to populate coding fields in a variety of discovery management software programs.

Generally, there is first a request for ESI from a defined time period. Second, there are requests for any and all ESI in native format, both existing and deleted. Third, there is typically a request for ESI from specific "key players."

Ostensibly, these requests are made to uncover relevant data, but at times requests may border on harassing. For example, requesting an overly broad time period for production of ESI. Depending on the nature and method used by your client for preservation of data, metadata may not always be readily available. For example, discovery requests often seek deleted ESI, which may impose additional efforts if also seeking the retrieval of corresponding metadata. For this reason, the discovery objections of overly broad and unduly burdensome discovery remain available to the producing party.

As with all discovery requests, the attorney-client privilege equally applies to ESI. This might be part of the electronic records strategy if there exists active involvement by in-house counsel or if "key players" actively and regularly sought counsel and advice from outside lawyers.

The Impact of Privacy Law on e-Discovery

The impact of privacy law on e-discovery depends on the nature of the case. For example, there is typically no impact on an employment case where the employee handbook explicitly states that there shall be no expectation of privacy with the use of work computers. However, there was a recent exception in the New Jersey state courts involving an employment case. An employee had used her work computer to access e-mails from her personal account, which were communications with her lawyer. The employer argued no expectation of privacy and that the privilege had been waived. The New Jersey court upheld the attorney-client privilege and precluded the discovery of those e-mail communications. Stengart v. Loving Care Agency Inc., 990 A.2d 650 (N.J. 2010).

During discovery the parties should, as a matter of course, agree to a confidentiality agreement early in the litigation. By doing so, parties may initially designate certain documents as "confidential" or even for "attorney's eyes only" upon their own assessment. Most confidentiality agreements permit subsequent challenges to a designation. However, having such an agreement in place can facilitate overall disclosure especially with documents of a potentially sensitive nature such as banking, medical, human resources, and security information since the parties have some assurance on the limitations of its disbursement.

Consequences of Violating e-Discovery Rules

The consequences of not disclosing relevant ESI during discovery include sanctions, either monetary or adverse inferences, on companies and possible sanctions on non-compliant lawyers.

For example, in Qualcomm Inc., v. Broadcom Corp., 2008 WL 66932, at *1 (S.D. Cal. Jan. 7, 2008), the court found clear and convincing evidence that Qualcomm intentionally withheld tens of thousands of e-mails and electronic documents to prevent the defendants from discovering information to support their affirmative defense of waiver in a patent infringement case. *Id.* at *6. The court further determined that Qualcomm's attorneys, either intentionally or with reckless disregard as to their discovery obligations, assisted in the discovery violations. *Id.* at *17. On remand, however, the court refused to impose sanctions against the attorneys individually due to a lack of bad faith. Qualcomm Inc., v. Broadcom Corp., 2010 WL 1336937, at *7 (S.D. Cal. Apr. 2, 2010). Overall, the court imposed sanctions against Qualcomm to cover the defendants' attorney fees and costs incurred during the litigation, totaling $8,568,633.24. *Qualcomm*, 2008 WL 66932, at *20.

Violations may be identified by opposing counsel or even by the court. An attorney can file for a review of undisclosed electronic records at any time, upon a showing to the court of why such action is merited.

Looking to the Future

I anticipate that the e-discovery process will become less onerous and less costly as technology adapts to facilitate the effort. However, that day has not yet arrived, and the quantity of ESI continues to multiply. There is almost not a single case that does not have some aspect of e-discovery. Over the next few years, some will embrace the new tools and advancements in this area, and some will continue to do what they have always done. The main change will be that the courts now expect that counsel have some proficiency with and understanding of e-discovery.

At the present time, costs, advancements in technology, and presence of ESI in most cases are increasing. If properly managed, however, these changes can help with ESI. For example, technology will help speed ESI review and sorting/culling capabilities. Going forward, there will be a greater expectation by the court that litigation will be affected by technology and electronic records management, especially as younger judges take the bench.

Final Thoughts

My advice to lawyers litigating cases involving e-discovery is simply this—the earlier that you can assess ESI, the better. You should utilize proactive preservation efforts from the beginning and follow up to ensure compliance with said directives. Early assessment allows the lawyer to focus on key issues in the case and not be distracted or sidetracked by discovery issues.

In order to achieve these goals, however, there must be improved communication with the client and knowledge of the IT aspect of the case.

Key Takeaways

- The first step in implementing an e-discovery strategy is a personal meeting with the client, and if possible, all "key players." It is extremely beneficial to meet with the IT staff of corporate clients to learn more about storage locations of ESI and retention policies. It is important to define the scope of potential ESI at each source, as well as the storage location.
- The earlier that you can assess ESI, the better. You should utilize proactive preservation efforts from the beginning and follow up to ensure compliance with said directives.

Related Resources

Cases that are relevant to the matters covered include the January 2010 opinion issued by federal district court Judge Scheindlin in the case of Pension Comm. of the Univ. of Montreal Pension Plan v. Banc of Am. Sec., L.L.C., 2010 WL 184312 (S.D.N.Y. Jan. 15, 2010). Most federal courts are now establishing local rules on ESI. For example, the federal district court for the Western District of Pennsylvania has revised its Fed. R. Civ. P. 26(f) Report of the Parties to address specifically ESI and related issues. The federal rules of civil procedure have specifically addressed ESI since December 2006.

- The Pension Comm. of the Univ. of Montreal Pension Plan v. Banc of Am. Sec., L.L.C., 2010 WL 184312 (S.D.N.Y. Jan. 15, 2010), *available at* http://www.ediscoverylaw.com/2010/01/articles/case-summaries/zubulake-revisited-six-years-later-judge-shira-scheindlin-issues-her-latest-ediscovery-opinion
- FED. R. CIV. P. 26(f), *available at* http://www.law.cornell.edu/rules/frcp/Rule26.htm

Joseph A. DiMenno is a shareholder of Dickie, McCamey & Chilcote PC. He concentrates his practice in the areas of commercial litigation, banking litigation, employment law, and health care law, with a particular emphasis in technology and electronic discovery matters.

Mr. DiMenno is a member of the Allegheny County Bar Association where he is also a member of the Hispanic Attorneys Committee. He is admitted to practice before the United States District Court for the Eastern, Middle, and Western Districts of Pennsylvania and United States Court of Appeals for the Third Circuit.

Additionally, he maintains a BV® Distinguished™ Peer Review Rating from Martindale-Hubbell and was named as a Pennsylvania Rising Star in Pennsylvania Super Lawyers.

Mr. DiMenno is active in The Arthritis Foundation for Western Pennsylvania as a board member and is a former president of the University of Pennsylvania Alumni Club of Western Pennsylvania. He also serves as a board member with the Pittsburgh History & Landmarks Foundation.

Mr. DiMenno graduated from University of Pennsylvania in 1991 with a B.A. in political science. He received his J.D. from University of Pittsburgh in 1995.

From Preservation to Production: The Dos and Don'ts of e-Discovery in Litigation

Michael C. Lasky and Marc J. Rachman

Partners

Davis & Gilbert LLP

ASPATORE

Regulations Governing Electronic Records and e-Discovery

For cases in federal court, the Federal Rules of Civil Procedure contain specific rules governing electronic records and discovery. For cases in state court, some state courts follow the rules set forth in the Federal Rules of Civil Procedure, but many do not, and either have their own rules governing electronic records and discovery or rely on court decisions on the subject.

Given the variations from state to state and between state procedure and the Federal Rules of Civil Procedure, we will focus on the Federal Rules of Civil Procedure in this chapter.

The Federal Rules of Civil Procedure

The Federal Rules of Civil Procedure were amended in 2006 to address e-discovery more specifically. The following new/modified rules concern electronically stored information (ESI) and e-discovery:

- Rule 16 – Concerning pretrial conferences and amending subsection 16(b) to address the handling of electronically stored information early in the litigation if such discovery is expected to occur.
- Rule 26 – General provisions governing discovery; subsection (f) now requires the parties to discuss discovery of ESI; subsection (b)(5)(B) now provides a mechanism by which parties may "claw back" inadvertently produced privileged information.
- Rule 33 – Concerning interrogatories, amended to parallel Rule 34(a) to address ESI.
- Rule 34 – Concerning requests for documents, amended to add "electronically stored information" to the types of documents/information a party may request; also added subsection (b)(1)(C) to allow parties to specify the form(s) in which ESI is to be produced; subsection (b)(2)(D) allowing a responding party to object to a requested form of production; and subsection (b)(2)(E)(ii) requiring a party to produce ESI in the form(s) in which it is ordinarily maintained or in a reasonably usable form.
- Rule 37 – Concerning sanctions for failure to make disclosures or cooperate in discovery; includes what has been popularly regarded

as a "safe harbor" limit on sanctions under Rule 37 for the loss of electronically stored information as a result of the routine operation of computer systems. [1]

- Rule 45 – Governing non-parties' obligations in responding to subpoenas for documents and corresponding to changes in Rules 26, 33, 37.

Table 1

Federal Rules of Evidence Concerning ESI

Federal Rule	Description
Rule 16 (b)(3)(B)(iii)	Pretrial Scheduling Order may provide for disclosure or discovery of ESI
Rule 26(b)(5)(B)	Party may assert claim of privilege or work product over information produced in discovery, triggering the receiving party's duty to return, sequester or destroy the information and refrain from use or disclosure until the claim is resolved.
Rule 26(f)(3)(c)	Parties must meet and confer and include issues about disclosure or discovery of ESI in their discovery plan.
Rule 33(d)	Response to interrogatories may be made by specifying records, including specifically ESI, that must be reviewed and allowing the interrogating party to inspect/audit/copy/ summarize the records.
Rule 34(b)(1)(C)	Request for production of documents may specify the form(s) in which ESI is to be produced.
Rule 34(B)(2)(D)	Party may object to request for production of ESI or requested form; party must state form(s) it intends to use.

[1] The Hon. Lee H. Rosenthal, Chair of the Committee that drafted the 2006 amendments to the Federal Rules, does not agree that Rule 37 is a true "safe harbor," as the limit on sanctions is preceded by the language "absent exceptional circumstances." "Electronic Discovery: Views from the Judges," 76 Fordham L. Rev. 1 (October 2007), p. 10.

Rule 34 (b)(2)(E)(ii)	If request for production of ESI does not specify form, a party must produce it in a form which is ordinarily maintained or in a reasonably useable form.
Rule 34 (b)(2)(E)(iii)	ESI only needs to be produced in one form.
Rule 37(e)	Court may not impose sanctions for failing to provide ESI lost as a result of a routine, good faith operation of an electronic information system absent exceptional circumstances.
Rule 45(d)(1)	Setting forth rules re ESI in context of non-party subpoenas, and providing that ESI from sources that are not reasonably accessible need not be produced.

Federal Rules of Evidence - Rule 502

Rule 502 of the Federal Rules of Evidence was added in 2008 to address, at least in part, the privilege review problem. It is also addressed, in part, in Rule 26(b)(5)(B).

The issue relates to the inadvertent disclosure of privileged materials, which in certain circumstances can lead to a waiver of the attorney-client or work product privilege. Potentially, such a waiver could lead to a subject matter privilege waiver, opening the door to discovery of other related privileged communications. Expensive and time-consuming privilege reviews are therefore necessary to minimize or eliminate the risk of a privilege waiver.

In order to address the friction between requiring voluminous productions of electronic records and the potential for inadvertent privilege waiver, Federal Rule of Evidence 502 was enacted. It provides that when inadvertent disclosure of privileged or work product material occurs in a federal proceeding or is made to a federal office or agency, the disclosure does not operate as a waiver of privilege in any proceeding (federal or state) provided that certain criteria are met. Specifically, the disclosure must be inadvertent and the privilege holder must take reasonable steps to prevent disclosure and promptly rectify the error. It also limits the effect of a privilege waiver resulting from inadvertent disclosure of privileged material in a state proceeding in a subsequent federal proceeding. Rule 502, together with the amendments to Rule 26, do not eliminate the need for a privilege review—many litigants are justifiably concerned that they will not be able to "unring the bell" if privileged information is disclosed—but they do provide parties producing voluminous information with some protection for errors in review or processing.

Need for Additional Regulation

One of the major e-discovery issues that demands further attention, though not necessarily further regulation, is proportionality. The time/money cost of exhaustively gathering, searching, and producing ESI can dwarf the amount in controversy in many cases. Additionally, ESI means that there is more metadata—"information about information"—available than ever before. A requesting party receiving, in a document production, a copy of a letter sent by U.S. mail will not have access to as much information about the letter as a requesting party who receives the Word version of the same letter in electronic format attached to an e-mail—e.g., time sent/received, creation and editing dates, tracked changes, etc. Also, with ESI, there are likely to be more copies or versions of a document than with hard copies. People tend to treat e-mail as a means of conversation, and given the ease with which an e-mail can be sent to many people at once, a company may find itself with dozens or even hundreds of copies of the same e-mail, all of which potentially could be responsive to a document request.

The costs and burdens of e-discovery are, therefore, factors that may be driving a perceived need for additional regulation.[2] However, it is not clear to these authors whether additional regulations would help to alleviate the burden of e-discovery on parties. Absent an outright ban on requesting information on backup tapes, or a legislated limit on the

[2] The costs start adding up even before documents are requested or collected for production. As discussed further below, a party who reasonably anticipates litigation has a duty to preserve all potentially relevant information. This can significantly add to a company's ESI management and storage costs. The fear of spoliation allegations and sanctions for failure to preserve ESI may even drive parties to preserve a far greater amount of ESI at greater cost than is necessary.

number of custodians whose e-mails would have to be searched in response to a request, neither of which are practical solutions, it is hard to see how additional rules will help parties cut down on the costs of preservation and production.

The principle of proportionality underlies the rules we already have. Assessing how much burden a party should bear in discovery, and how big a burden needs to be before it is considered "undue," necessarily varies from case to case. What is excessive in a $25,000 dispute may be more than reasonable in a multi-million dollar dispute. Moreover, there is flexibility in the current regulations that provide protections to a producing party—e.g., the broad term ESI; the fact that the definition of "inaccessible" data is subject to interpretation in every case; the ability of the courts to fashion remedies (e.g., cost-shifting) where discovery costs and burden threaten to spin out of control, etc.

Additionally, there is always the possibility that technological advances will make any more specific, bright-line rules obsolete. For example, in 2003 and 2004, when the seminal *Zubulake* decisions concerning e-discovery were issued, Zubulake v. UBS Warburg LLC, 216 F.R.D. 280 (S.D.N.Y. 2003); Zubulake v. UBS Warburg LLC, 217 F.R.D. 309 (S.D.N.Y. 2003); Zubulake v. UBS Warburg LLC, 220 F.R.D. 212 (S.D.N.Y. 2003); Zubulake v. UBS Warburg LLC, 229 F.R.D. 422 (S.D.N.Y. 2003), backup tapes were generally considered inaccessible, and in most cases, far too expensive to restore and search. Since then, litigants have generally assumed that a request for backup tapes will lead to an arduous and expensive restoration project requiring cost-shifting. Yet, technological advances have allowed companies to engage in a more dynamic data backup process in many companies, and backup records are no longer necessarily offline, kept on inaccessible tapes. This is one of the reasons that the term "backup tape" is not found in the 2006 amendments to the Federal Rules.[3]

[3] See "Electronic Discovery: Views from the Bench," 76 Fordham L. Rev. 1 (Oct. 2007), including commentary by the Hon. Lee Rosenthal, United States District Court Judge for the Southern District of Texas in Houston, who also served on and became chair of the Judicial Conference Advisory Committee for Rules of Civil Procedure, which promulgated the 2006 changes to the Rules. Judge Rosenthal states that the term "backup tapes" was not included in the final version of the amended rules. As she explained, "Backup tapes, which had been these big, ungainly things that were not indexed or searchable, now are smaller and often searchable." Id., p. 7.

Certain judges—notably the Hon. Shira Scheindlin of the United States District Court for the Southern District of New York (who decided *Zubulake*) and the Hon. Lee Rosenthal of the United States District Court for the Southern District of Texas (who chaired the committee charged with drafting amendments to the Federal Rules of Civil Procedure)—have taken a leading role in providing clarity to litigants concerning the scope of their electronic discovery obligations, including the extent of their obligation to preserve documents once they reasonably anticipate litigation. As eager as litigants are for easy-to-follow rules of do's and don'ts for preservation and production, these leading jurists have expressed their reluctance to set absolute standards.

In fact, Judge Scheindlin qualified her recent decision concerning sanctions for e-discovery failures in Pension Comm. of Univ. of Montreal Pension Plan v. Banc of Am. Sec. LLC, 2010 WL 184312 (Jan. 1, 2010). In an opinion related to e-discovery in this case, she stated: "I stress that at the end of the day the judgment call of whether to award sanctions [for discovery failures] is inherently subjective…while it would be helpful to develop a list of relevant criteria a court should review in evaluating discovery conduct, *these inquiries are inherently fact intensive and must be reviewed case by case.*" *Id.* At *7. (Emphasis added.) Judge Scheindlin then went on to list discovery failures that would support a finding of gross negligence when a duty to preserve documents has arisen. This guidance is certainly helpful and should be taken into account when faced with a document preservation obligation. Judge Scheindlin listed the following failures in support of her finding that certain plaintiffs had engaged in gross negligence with respect to their preservation duties:

- Failure to issue a written litigation hold
- Failure to identify key players and ensure their electronic and paper records are preserved
- Failure to cease deletion of e-mail in the face of a preservation obligation
- Failure to preserve former employee records that are in a party's possession, custody, or control
- Failure to preserve backup tapes when they are the sole source of relevant information or relate to key players

As useful as this information is, there is a risk that parties may interpret them as new "bright-line" rules, compliance with which means safety from sanctions, and violation of which always leads to dire consequences. This, however, is not how the decision should be read. A plaintiff's idea of the key players may be different from a defendant's idea. Moreover, what should or should not be a sanctionable e-discovery failure often depends on the facts of a given case. For example, in Rimkus Consulting Group Inc. v. Cammarata, 2010 WL 645253 (S.D. Tex., Feb. 19, 2010) decided February 19, 2010 by the Hon. Lee H. Rosenthal, the Court held that certain sanctions were not appropriate for anything short of intentional misconduct—in contrast to *Pension Committee*, in which severe sanctions (an adverse jury instruction) were ordered where the parties were found to have been grossly negligent. Judge Rosenthal noted that, on the *Rimkus* record, there was "conflicting evidence about the reasons the defendants deleted the e-mails and attachments; evidence that some of the deleted e-mails and attachments were favorable to defendants, and an extensive amount of other evidence for the plaintiff to use."

These two cases illustrate the problem with boiling the sophisticated, lengthy reasoning in these decisions down to a list of "do's" and "don'ts"—such a list may provide false comfort, or encourage pursuit of sanctions where no real harm occurred. The real issue is not always whether there was or was not a particular e-discovery failure that can be checked off a list, but whether it made any real difference in the case, and whether the producing party took reasonable steps in the face of the request(s) seeking the production of ESI.

Key Players in Changing the e-Discovery Rules

The key e-discovery-related amendments to the Federal Rules of Civil Procedure were the result of work by the Standing Committee on the Rules of Practice and Procedure of the Judicial Conference and the Civil Rules Advisory Committee. Additionally, e-discovery rules and regulations are evolving in part because of the challenges that parties face responding to discovery.

Some judges are also deeply involved in this area. The Hon. Shira Scheindlin and the Hon. Lee Rosenthal, whose recent e-discovery decisions are discussed briefly above, are recognized as leading jurists in e-discovery.

The Sedona Conference has also done considerable important work in this field—work on which many judges have relied in analyzing parties' efforts to preserve and produce responsive documents. The Sedona Conference is a nonprofit organization, whose mission is "to allow leading jurists, lawyers, experts, academics, and others, at the cutting edge of issues in the area of antitrust law, complex litigation, and intellectual property rights, to come together—in conferences and mini-think tanks (Working Groups)." www.sedonaconference.org. Principles and commentaries issued by the Sedona Conference are frequently cited by the courts. See, for example, the *Zubulake* decisions by Judge Scheindlin. Some of the key Sedona Conference publications in this area are:

- Commentary on Inactive Information Sources (July, 2009)
- Commentary on Preservation, Management and Identification of Sources of Information that are Not Reasonably Accessible (August, 2008)
- Commentary on Non-Party Production and Rule 45 Subpoenas (April, 2008)
- Commentary on Legal Holds (August, 2007)

All of these may be found online at: http://www.thesedonaconference.org/content/miscFiles/publications_html?grp=wgs110

Intent of Legal Standards in e-Discovery

The discovery standards in the Federal Rules of Civil Procedure show an intent to balance litigants' needs for full disclosure of all information relevant to any claim or defense with the need to protect responding parties from disproportionate burden and expense.

The basic principle governing all discovery, including e-discovery, is found in Rule 26(b)(1):

> Unless otherwise limited by court order, the scope of discovery is as follows: Parties may obtain discovery regarding any non-privileged matter that is relevant to any party's claim or defense—including the existence,

> description, nature, custody, condition and location of any documents or other tangible things and the identity and location of persons who know of any discoverable matter…Relevant information need not be admissible at the trial if the discovery appears reasonably calculated to lead to discovery of admissible evidence.

The same limitations apply in the e-discovery sphere as with any other discovery, and proportionality is the key consideration. Indeed, Rule 26(b)(2)(C) requires courts to limit the frequency or extent of discovery if it is cumulative, duplicative, can be obtained from another source that is more convenient, less burdensome, or less expensive, or if the burden or expense of the proposed discovery outweighs its likely benefit, considering the needs of the case, the amount in controversy, the parties' resources, the importance of the issues at stake in the action, and the importance of the discovery in resolving the issues.

Balancing the need for relevant information with the burden of obtaining that information also underlies the amendments to Rule 16 and 26(f), as parties are now required to meet and confer early in a litigation concerning any issues about disclosure or discovery of ESI, including the form or forms in which it should be produced.

e-Discovery Strategies

The below discussion is predicated on the assumption that a party's goal is to obtain proportionate, thorough discovery to flesh out all the real issues in a dispute, avoid needlessly costly pitfalls, and get as efficiently as possible to settlement, summary judgment, or trial. As the recent *Pension Committee* and *Rimkus* decisions show, however, serious potential traps for litigants lie in the preservation of documents, before discovery even begins in earnest. Thus, this discussion focuses particularly on preservation issues.

Components of an E-Discovery Strategy

The components of an e-discovery strategy can be described in a few simple steps, but of course, the devil is in the details:

1. Know what information you have that may be relevant to any party's claims or defenses.

2. Preserve it in a timely manner,[4] and diligently follow up.
3. Identify the information you need to support your claims and defenses.
4. If you have it, produce it. If you do not, go and get it through discovery.

Many an expensive and painful discovery dispute has arisen because a party failed to identify relevant information before it was lost or migrated to an inaccessible (or only expensively accessible) location. If e-mails are currently accessible on a company's server, a snapshot of relevant accounts should be taken now rather than risking loss of the e-mails, or having to retrieve them from backup tapes down the road.[5] Moreover, understanding the documents you already have is necessary to formulate requests for documents from parties and/or to determine if documents will need to be obtained from third parties.

Thus, the first step—knowing what you have—is critical to designing a proper document preservation strategy and the cornerstone for building an overall discovery strategy.[6]

A good understanding of the sources of ESI, and the methods and costs associated with retrieval of ESI, are key to formulating objections to discovery requests or opposing motions to compel production. Judges are not likely to grant a protective order or deny a motion to compel production of ESI based on a party's assertion of cost and burden alone. However, a requesting party may be required to pay costs of retrieval/processing (cost-shifting), or

---

[4] As noted above, the duty to preserve evidence is triggered by either the filing of a lawsuit or even earlier if a party has notice that future litigation is likely. *See, e.g., Cache La Poudre Feeds LLC v. Land O' Lakes Inc.* 244 F.R.D. 614 (D. Colorado, 2007) (discussing when the preservation duty arose, and concluding that, while the duty may arise when a party has notice that future litigation is likely, "something more than an equivocal statement of discontent" is required).

[5] A party can lose a cost-shifting argument, however, if an expensive restoration/retrieval process would not have been needed if the party had properly preserved accessible documents once the duty to preserve arose. *See, e.g., Peskoff v. Faber*, 251 F.R.D. 59 (D. Columbia, 2008) (because defendant failed to preserve e-mails and allowed auto-deletion process to continue after duty to preserve arose, costs of expensive forensic examination would not be shifted to the requesting party); *Quinby v. WestLB AG,* 245 FRD 94 (SDNY, 2006) (party not entitled to shift the costs of restoring and searching data that it converted into an inaccessible format at a time when it should have anticipated litigation).

[6] Attached as an appendix is a checklist for attorneys guiding their clients' document preservation efforts

discovery may be denied if a party can make a strong showing that the burden is disproportionate to the claims in the case.

The second step of preservation is critical to avoid expensive and potentially disastrous distractions from the ultimate dispute in a given case. Parties may have legitimate objections (relevance, privilege, burden, expense, etc.) to requests for discovery. A party that has properly preserved documents can fight a motion to compel production of ESI to which it has objected. If it loses, it can produce the ESI as ordered by the court and live to fight another day. However, if the ESI has been destroyed in the meantime—intentionally, negligently, or otherwise—the failure to preserve documents can potentially be a case killer.

Notably, failure to preserve documents led to sanctions in both the *Pension Committee* and *Rimkus* cases discussed above. In *Pension Committee*, 2010 WL 184312, thirteen plaintiffs were found to have been at least negligent in their efforts to meet their discovery obligations. All were required to pay monetary sanctions, and the Court determined that it would issue an adverse inference instruction to the jury for the six worst offenders. The jury would then be permitted, but not required, to find that the lost or destroyed evidence would have been favorable to the defendants. Judge Scheindlin noted that, had she found the plaintiffs deliberately destroyed documents, even harsher sanctions could have ensued, from an instruction to the jury that it *must* assume the lost or destroyed documents were relevant and favorable to the defendant, to dismissal of the plaintiffs' case in its entirety. In *Rimkus*, 2010 WL 645253 *32, Judge Rosenthal noted in her analysis that, while some loss of documents had occurred due to the defendants' deletion of them, the damage was "far from irreparable" because the defendants had produced some of the documents, and Rimkus had been able to obtain deleted records from other sources. *Id.* At *34. Thus, Judge Rosenthal concluded that the most extreme sanction—default judgment or dismissal—was not appropriate, but due to the defendants' intentional destruction of documents after the duty to preserve had arisen, a form of adverse inference instruction would be given. *Id.*

For the third and fourth steps—identifying information you need and producing it or seeking discovery to get it—a consideration must be given to metadata. In some cases, metadata can be of minimal importance. In others, it can be critical. If there could be an issue as to when an e-mail was sent or received, if it was read, whether a document was copied or modified, and if so, how and when, who wrote and commented on a document, when an invoice was transmitted, etc., then serious consideration should be given to demanding that documents be produced or to producing documents in native file format.[7] If producing electronically-stored documents that are in part privileged, or contain irrelevant information concerning other products or clients, it may be wiser to produce them in searchable TIFF or PDF form[8] with redactions, providing appropriate metadata fields, in a discovery database such as Concordance or Summation. Below is a table showing examples of the various different file types in which ESI may be stored.

Table 2

Example File Types

File Extension	Description
Archives	
.7z	Archived File
.zip	Archived File
.rar	Archived File

[7] Native file format means the default file format a computer program uses to store data on a drive or disk. For example, a Word document is saved to a drive or disk as a Word file (with a .doc file name extension) and producing it in native file format means producing it as a Word file, rather than as a printed hard copy document, pdf, or other formatted file. The recipient can then open the document on his or her computer using Word. Depending on the e-mail program, e-mails may be saved, with their attachments and data concerning their transmission, in a compressed file. For Microsoft Outlook, this is usually a .pst file. Again, the recipient of a native file format production of e-mails in .pst files can load those documents onto his/her computer, and view them in the Microsoft Outlook program.

[8] TIFF (Tagged Image File Format) and PDF (Portable Document Format) files are types of "petrified" electronic documents. One way to think of them is the equivalent of a photocopy, except viewable on a computer screen. These types of files may be made so that they are searchable, or so that a user can sort them by metadata fields such as sender, recipient, date sent/received, etc. A Word document or e-mail produced as a TIFF or PDF file may be scrubbed of metadata, or redacted. The advantage of TIFF and PDF files is that they cannot be edited, they are viewable on most computers even if the recipient does not have the same proprietary software (such as Microsoft Word, Photoshop, or QuickBooks) and the recipient will not be able to see any redacted material; however, since they can be scrubbed of all metadata or produced with selected metadata only, and sorting/organizing them may require specific case management software, a requesting party may have a preference for native file format where possible.

Databases	
.dat	DOS Basic
.mdb	Microsoft Access
.nsf	Lotus Notes database
Personal Information Manager	
.msg	Microsoft Outlook manager
.pst	Microsoft Outlook email communication
.mbox	Apple Outlook manager
Documents	
.csv	Ascii text encoded as comma separated values
.doc	Microsoft Word
.docx	Microsoft Office Word 2007 for Windows/2008 for Mac
.html	Hypertext Markup Language
.pdf	Portable Document Format
.rtf	Rich Text Format
.txt	Wordperfect document
.wpd	Microsoft Works document
.wps	Microsoft PowerPoint Presentation
.ppt	Office Open XML Presentation
.pptx	Office Open XML Presentation
.xls	Microsoft Excel spreadsheet
.xlsx	Office Open CML worksheet sheet
.123	Lotus Notes 1-2-3
Graphics	
.bmp	Microsoft Windows bitmap formated image
.jpeg	Image format widely used to display photographic images
.gif	Graphics Interchange Format

.png	Portable Network Graphic
.psd	Adobe photoshop drawing
.tiff	Tagg Image File Format
Sound, Music, Video	
.wav	Sound/Music file
.wma	Sound/Music file
.mp3	Sound/Music file
.avi	Sound/Music file
.flv	Video file
.mov	Video file
.mpeg	Video file
.wmv	Video file
.swf	Video file

In all cases, the revised Federal Rules of Civil Procedure mandate that the parties confer regarding the method of production for ESI. In *Covad Communications Co. v. Revonet Inc.*, 254 F.R.D. 147 (D. Columbia, 2008), a dispute concerning the alleged conversion and misappropriation of trade secrets, the parties found themselves in a dispute over the form of production of e-mails. The defendant had already produced the e-mails at issue in hard copy form, and the plaintiff demanded they be produced in native form. In *Covad,* the initial hard copy production had been made before the revised Federal Rules took effect, but the court noted that the defendant was "playing with fire" by producing the e-mails only in hard copy form in light of *Zubulake* and other e-discovery decisions. Ultimately, the parties were required to split the costs of having a paralegal remove privileged e-mails from the native file format collection of e-mails. The court said: "Since both parties went through the same stop sign, it appears to me that they both should pay for the crash. . . . I would hope that my decision will have a didactic purpose. This whole controversy could have been eliminated had Covad asked for the data in native format in the first place or had Revonet asked Covad in what format it wanted the data before it presumed that it was not native." The court's decision and order illustrates not only the wisdom of conferring regarding the method of production of ESI, but also the courts' impatience with avoidable discovery disputes on the issue.

When e-Discovery is Critical to the Case Being Litigated

There are few cases anymore in which e-discovery is not a significant part of the discovery process, if not a critical one. Below are listed different types of cases and situations that may arise in litigation, and the ways in which e-discovery can be a critical part of discovery in them.

<u>Employment Discrimination</u>

E-discovery often proves to be a critical part of an employment discrimination case. Using the example of where a company is accused of discrimination by a former employee, if the offending supervisors' e-mails contain discriminatory comments about the employee or others in his or her protected class, it could be "game over" for the employer. Or, conversely, if the employee's e-mail account or browser history at work contains evidence that he or she spent all day on non-work related projects, or forwarded the employer's confidential and proprietary information to a competitor, an employer's legitimate business reasons for terminating that employee may go from plausible to indisputable.

Indeed, Zubulake v. UBS Warburg, 217 F.R.D. 309 (S.D.N.Y. 2003), which provided the forum for Judge Scheindlin's much-cited e-discovery opinions, was a gender discrimination lawsuit. The plaintiff had requested that the defendant produce all documents concerning any communications by or between UBS employees concerning the plaintiff. After UBS produced documents, the plaintiff knew that UBS had not produced all such communications because she herself was in possession of more such documents than UBS had produced. The court ordered restoration of UBS's archival media and searches and deferred a determination on cost-shifting until after this was completed. After the restoration effort, during which it was revealed that some e-mails and archives had been destroyed, Judge Scheindlin found that UBS was in violation of its document preservation duties. Zubulake v. UBS Warburg, 220 F.R.D. 212 (S.D.N.Y. 2003). The Court did not order an adverse inference instruction, but did order the defendant to bear the plaintiff's costs to re-depose certain witnesses to inquire into destruction of evidence and concerning newly discovered e-mails.[9] After this was done, the plaintiff moved again for sanctions, which were granted, as the court found that UBS had failed to locate, preserve, and timely produce information and sanctioned UBS for over $200,000 in costs. Zubulake v. UBS Warburg, 229 F.R.D. 422 (S.D.N.Y. 2004).[10]

Another example is Jackson v. Planco, 660 F. Supp. 2d 562 (E.D. Pa. 2009), which was a disability discrimination and retaliation case. In *Jackson*, the defendant employer moved for summary judgment and won. ESI played a critical role as the employer had evidence of the employee's Web browsing history, showing that the employee violated its Internet policies by viewing gun Web sites at the office.

Restrictive Covenants

Another type of case where e-discovery can be critical is one involving claims relating to an employee's restrictive covenants. For example, *Rimkus*, 2010 WL 645253 (discussed above), involved restrictive covenants. The ESI at issue concerned former employees discussing leaving Rimkus to start a new, competing company, and taking/using Rimkus' confidential information to do so. It is not hard to imagine how an e-mail trail or metadata showing when particular documents were copied or accessed by former employees accused of competing unfairly with their former employer or violating their restrictive covenants could affect the outcome of a case.

[9] Although the Court held that the costs for searches and retrieval of inaccessible ESI—*i.e.*, backup tapes—should usually be borne by the requesting party, given UBS's conduct, UBS had to bear three-quarters of the $166,000 estimated costs to restore backup tapes, and all of the estimated $108,000 costs to review documents on those tapes. *Zubulake,* 216 FRD 280 (S.D.N.Y. 2003).

[10] The sanctions that were awarded included: (1) paying for re-deposition of relevant UBS personnel and other witnesses concerning new materials produced from backup tapes; (2) paying the costs of restoration and production of relevant documents from backup tapes; (3) an adverse inference instruction to the jury; and (4) paying the plaintiff's reasonable costs and attorney's fees for the sanctions motions. Additionally, the Court noted that UBS also had a "self-executing sanction" because the newly discovered e-mails seemed to contradict testimony of a UBS employee who had not had the benefit of reviewing these e-mails before his first deposition, and the plaintiff would be allowed, of course, to use that testimony at trial. *Id.*, 437, 439-440.

Misappropriation of Trade Secrets

ESI can be used to show that trade secrets were appropriately protected, or to show that they had been shared and used in a manner that destroys their trade secret protection. For example, in Lockheed Martin Corp. v. L-3 Communications Integrated Sys., 2010 WL 1891779 (N.D. Ga. 2010), the court tossed out a $37.3 million trade secrets verdict for Lockheed Martin Corp. and ordered a new trial after finding that Lockheed had failed to turn over relevant e-mails concerning use of its purported trade secrets by another company without compensation to Lockheed. The court held that the defendant L-3 had been deprived of its opportunity to make the argument to the jury that the trade secret status of the proprietary information at issue had terminated when Lockheed allowed the other company to use it without compensation. The Court held that a terminating sanction was not appropriate because the harm to L-3 could be fixed by a new trial.

Copyright Infringement and Other Intellectual Property Matters

ESI can also prove critical in copyright infringement cases. For example, in Columbia Pictures, Inc. v. Bunnell, 2007 WL 4877701 (C.D. Cal., Dec. 13, 2007), a copyright infringement case, the court granted a default judgment due to spoliation of electronic evidence. This case concerned the defendants' alleged participation in illegal downloading and file sharing of copyrighted works (movies) produced by the plaintiffs. ESI was critical: the plaintiffs needed full IP addresses to determine the full extent of the infringement and whether the defendants had actually infringed themselves. The defendants denied maintaining those records, but forum postings between moderators of the defendants' Web site referred to full IP addresses. The plaintiffs were able to show that the defendants "engaged in widespread and systematic efforts to destroy evidence" and "provided false testimony under oath in an effort to hide evidence of such destruction." After analyzing lesser sanctions such as exclusion of evidence or an adverse jury instruction, the Court found that the circumstances of the case were "sufficiently extraordinary" to merit the sanction of default judgment, as "lesser sanctions would not be adequate to punish the defendants for the wrongful conduct and ameliorate the prejudice and harm to the plaintiffs."

In Capitol Records, Inc. v. MP3Tunes, LLC, 261 F.R.D. 44 (S.D.N.Y. 2009), the parties hotly contested a number of e-discovery issues. Defendant MP3Tunes operated Web sites providing users with access to third party Web sites from which they could stream and listen to music and "sideload" music to a permanent "locker" assigned to them at www.MP3tunes.com. ESI was key to this dispute. The parties disagreed on the keyword search terms to use in MP3Tunes' e-mails. Ultimately, MP3Tunes was ordered to search for thirty different keywords in the e-mails of both senior and lower-level employees. MP3Tunes also sought to compel production of e-mails from plaintiffs, who argued that the e-mails were inaccessible. The court denied MP3Tunes' request, stating: "The day undoubtedly will come when burden arguments based on a large organization's lack of internal e-discovery software will be received about as well as the contention that a party should be spared from retrieving paper documents because it had filed them sequentially, but in no apparent groupings, in an effort to avoid the added expense of file folders or indices." However, the court still found the requested e-mails to be inaccessible, and limited what the plaintiffs would be required to search and produce.

ESI can also be critical in intellectual property cases where there is an issue over the creation date of the defendant's allegedly infringing work. The metadata of an e-mail or electronic document can be the linchpin in establishing or knocking out a defense of independent creation. ESI can also be critical for a plaintiff in a copyright case to establish that the defendant had access to the plaintiff's copyrighted work.

For example, American Express Co. v. Goetz, 515 F. 3d 156 (2d Cir. 2008), was a trademark infringement case concerning Amex's "MY LIFE. MY CARD." advertising campaign. In affirming the district court's grant of summary judgment to Amex, the Second Circuit held that the district court had not abused its discretion in determining that Goetz should not be permitted to engage in "wholesale rummaging" through Amex's electronic records, but only to electronic records pertaining to documents concerning the trademark at issue for which the dates of creation were in question.

Personal Injury

ESI is growing in importance in personal injury cases as well. Text messaging and BlackBerry or iPhone records may show that a driver accused of negligence was preoccupied in the moments leading up to an accident. Similarly, a plaintiff featured in a video or pictures of herself dancing at a party may undercut her claim that her injury has had an impact on her enjoyment of life.

For example, in Sedie v. U.S.A., 2010 WL 1644252 (N.D. Cal. Apr. 21, 2010), a plaintiff's MySpace page postings had a serious impact on his award in a personal injury case. Sedie sought $2.5 million in damages for the "hell on earth" he alleged his life had become after an accident with a U.S. Postal Service truck. He claimed he could no longer take part in activities he used to enjoy, such as painting and outdoor activities. However, on his MySpace page, well after the accident, he had a posting stating that he had recently been painting. He ended up getting a judgment in the case for far less than what he had claimed.

Protecting Electronic Information During Litigation

The key steps lawyers can take to protect ESI during litigation are:

1. Educate yourself early on your client's document retention protocols and capabilities.
2. Communicate immediately upon an action being initiated, or earlier if possible, to the client their duty to preserve ESI, and identify to the client any document retention protocols that should be modified or suspended.
3. Make appropriate secure copies of ESI that might be relevant to the litigation as early on as possible in the litigation, and make backup copies as well that are maintained separately from the initial copies.
4. Maintain clear records of the chain of custody of the preservation of the ESI and the efforts taken to preserve.
5. Regularly follow-up in writing with the client to remind them of their preservation obligations and to insure that they have implemented steps to preserve the appropriate ESI.

It is not only important to protect ESI during litigation (or even before, if a party reasonably anticipates litigation), it is essential. The penalties for failing to comply with document preservation obligations can be severe and can derail a case. At a minimum, e-discovery disputes concerning a failure to preserve documents can distract from the issues in dispute and hamper a case's progress. At worst, a party who fails to preserve relevant documents may be sanctioned by the court. As noted below, sanctions can range from monetary penalties to dismissal of a party's case altogether.

An important step after identifying sources of potentially relevant ESI is determining which sources should be copied or "petrified" so that the ESI is available and intact when it is needed. In some cases, imaging a particular employee's computer hard drive may be necessary. Or, an image of a folder on a company's shared network drive pertaining to the client account at issue may be appropriate.

With regard to e-mails, if a reasonable subset of the e-mails existing on a server can be identified, it is often useful to save that subset in one or several .pst files on DVDs or external hard drives to avoid the possibility of accidental deletion.

One litigant recently learned the hard way that failure to back up a flash drive before sending it for analysis could have severe consequences. In Wilson v. Thorn Energy LLC, 2010 WL 1712236 (S.D.N.Y Mar. 15, 2010), the plaintiffs made loans to and investments in the defendants' petroleum-related projects in Africa, and the defendants agreed to provide an accounting of their use of the plaintiff's funds. However, the defendants kept their only copies of certain documents necessary for the accounting on a USB flash drive. The USB drive failed, however, even before the promise to provide an accounting happened but after litigation had commenced, and the defendants discarded it. The defendants' attempt to rely on the "safe harbor" provision of Fed. R. Civ. P. 37 (e) (concerning loss of data as a result of good faith, routine operation of an electronic information system) failed, and sanctions ensued—specifically, the defendants were precluded at trial from offering evidence of their financial records or the data allegedly contained on the USB drive. This case clearly illustrates the need to adequately preserve ESI—including by making backup copies of important documents.

The Impact of Failing to Preserve ESI

The most obvious way a failure to preserve and protect ESI can affect the outcome of a litigation is sanctions. Sanctions for spoliation may include attorneys' fees (for conducting depositions or non-party or other discovery to locate alternate sources of "lost" documents, and/or for motion practice concerning spoliation); shifting the costs of locating and reviewing information to the opposing party (particularly for inaccessible sources of ESI, such as backup tapes, the costs for which are usually borne by the requesting party); adverse inference instructions to the jury; or even dismissal.

In *Rimkus*, 2010 WL 645253, employees who preemptively sued their former employer to challenge their restrictive covenants were sanctioned for spoliation of evidence. The Court held that the most severe sanctions—granting default judgment, striking pleadings, or giving adverse inference instructions—might not be imposed without evidence of the spoliators' "bad faith."

In TR Investors, LLC v. Genger, 2009 WL 4696062 (Del. Ch. Dec. 9, 2009), the defendant Genger, who was a director of the corporation, together with his computer consultant, intentionally destroyed all information on the unallocated space of a corporation's computer database using wiping software called "SecureClean." Genger did this despite a court order that enjoined the destruction of any company-related documents. The court sanctioned him. As to any affirmative defense or counterclaim he raised, Genger would have to meet an evidentiary burden one level higher than would otherwise be applicable—"clear and convincing" standard instead of by mere preponderance of the evidence. Furthermore, because Genger's conduct had so seriously compromised his integrity and credibility, he would not be able to rely on his own testimony alone to meet this burden.

Finally, in Goodman v. Praxair Services Inc., 632 F. Supp. 2d 494 (D. Md. 2009), the plaintiff contractor moved for spoliation sanctions based on the corporate defendant's destruction of an employee's laptop. The court found that the corporation willfully destroyed a laptop knowing that it contained evidence relevant to the contractor's claim, including e-mail correspondence, in violation of its duty to preserve evidence. Sanctions were not awarded based on the destruction of other companies' computers, however, because there was insufficient evidence that the materials on those computers were relevant to the contractor's claim.

As technology advances, ESI storage capacities will continue to grow and develop, making ESI storage less and less costly and more and more accessible. Attorneys must make themselves familiar with how clients store their information at the outset of any litigation. It is no longer enough to know where the boxes are stored. Now, key employees who created and/or accessed potentially relevant ESI, and information technology professionals who understand the company's ESI storage capabilities and systems, must be interviewed and involved in a company's preservation efforts.

Due to the sheer volume of ESI produced and stored in the ordinary course of business, attorneys must also become familiar with clients' document retention protocols and counsel them on development and adherence to such protocols.

Despite the many recent decisions there are addressing ESI, the courts do not appear to be moving in a new direction. The *Pension Committee* decision, for example, affirms the preservation obligations that parties already had. However, courts are becoming less tolerant of lapses in preservation efforts and are imposing higher expectations on parties to meet, confer, and develop rational, defensible strategies for preservation, collection, and production of ESI.

Key Takeaways

- In order to protect ESI during litigation, attorneys need to educate themselves early on about their client's document retention protocols and capabilities. They need to communicate immediately upon an action being initiated, or earlier if possible, to the client their duty to preserve ESI, and identify to the client any document retention protocols that should be modified or suspended.
- The attorney should make appropriate secure copies of ESI that might be relevant to the litigation as early on as possible in the litigation, and make backup copies as well that are maintained separately from the initial copies.
- The attorney should maintain clear records of the chain of custody of the preservation of the ESI and the efforts taken to preserve, and regularly follow up in writing with the client to remind them of their preservation obligations and to insure that they have implemented steps to preserve the appropriate ESI.

Michael C. Lasky *is a partner and co-chair of the Litigation Practice Group of Davis & Gilbert LLP. With more than thirty years of litigation experience, he has litigated a broad range of disputes involving complex commercial disputes relating to the purchase and sale of businesses, trade secret matters, intellectual property, the purchase and sale of business, and employment disputes. Mr. Lasky has also handled some of the leading New York cases involving the movement of talent between competitive companies. Electronic discovery and management of electronic records have been a prominent part of many of the litigations handled by Mr. Lasky. He is also a frequent author and speaker on issues affecting financial services and marketing communications. Mr. Lasky is a Phi Beta Kappa and honors graduate of Rutgers College and Rutgers Law School Newark, where he served as editor-in-chief of the* Rutgers Law Review.

Marc J. Rachman *is a partner in the Litigation Practice Group of Davis & Gilbert LLP and represents clients in a wide variety of complex commercial litigations. His litigation practice focuses on intellectual property litigation, including trademark and copyright infringement, false advertising, entertainment, right of public city, and domain name disputes. In counseling clients, he has developed document retention policies and electronic media retention protocols. Mr. Rachman has argued appeals before the U.S. Court of Appeals for the Second and Ninth Circuits and the Appellate Division of the New York State Supreme Court. He is the author of several articles relating to intellectual property and e-discovery matters and has spoken on various topics, including Social Media, Trademark Law, and the Federal Rules of Evidence. Mr. Rachman is a 1993 cum laude graduate from Boston University School of Law.*

Acknowledgment: *The authors would like to acknowledge Cheryl M. Plambeck, without whose significant contribution this chapter would not have been possible.*

Cheryl M. Plambeck *is an associate in the Litigation Practice Group of Davis & Gilbert LLP. Her practice involves litigation in both federal and state courts, covering a broad range of general commercial matters, including employment issues, contractual disputes, business torts, and media law. She has defended various corporate clients and their executives in sex, age, disability and other employment discrimination cases. Ms. Plambeck graduated with distinction from both McGill Law School in 2000, where she earned her B.C.L. and LL.B., and from Tulane Law School with her LL.M. (international and comparative law).*

Evolving Technology and Strategies in the Area of e-Discovery

Alison A. Grounds

Of Counsel

Troutman Sanders LLP

ASPATORE

Introduction

I am an attorney in our litigation section who specializes in matters related to e-discovery. Several years ago, we formed a dedicated practice team that focuses on e-discovery issues – The Electronic Discovery and Data Management Team; I am the head and one of the founders of that team. We realized that the constantly-evolving changes in this area, in rules, case law, and technology, warranted the undivided attention of one of our attorneys—and that lucky individual was me.

I became interested in e-discovery early in my career through our representation of a large pharmaceutical company in a false advertising matter. In that case, I led our efforts to sift through a data-dump produced by the other side, and coordinated our own efforts to collect, review, and produce large volumes of electronically stored information. I worked with outside vendors and the client to find the appropriate technology to help efficiently manage such volumes. The case was on an expedited discovery schedule that required our team to find the appropriate technological tools to help us review and analyze these large volumes for production and to isolate key documents for depositions, briefing, and use at a preliminary injunction hearing. By using the appropriate tools, we were able to perform targeted searches and craft queries to isolate key documents. The technology was not perfect and it has come a long way since those early cases, but I enjoyed the problem solving and investigation involved in using the appropriate tools for search and retrieval and in developing a project management plan that made the piles of data turn into the key tools for the case.

After my work on this case, I began to transition my focus from Intellectual Property litigation to a focus on e-discovery for all matters, including products liability cases, patent infringement matters, commercial disputes, class actions, labor and employment matters, and governmental investigations. My current role in the firm is to serve as an internal consultant for all of our attorneys and offices in relation to e-discovery issues, as well as any of our clients that face these issues in litigation, government investigations, or regulatory matters. I also consult with clients about data management issues and litigation readiness. I work with other members of our Electronic Discovery and Data Management team, including our litigation technology department, to develop best practices for the management of e-discovery, including evaluation of emerging technology and tools and selection of preferred vendors. I also work with our team to coordinate staffing and workflows for the collection, review, analysis, and production of electronically stored information. My primary focus is on e-discovery strategies and techniques, and making e-discovery a useful resource for our clients rather than just a burdensome cost.

Many of the larger law firms have formed similar groups and resources dedicated to e-discovery, and there are boutique firms that do nothing but consult on e-discovery and data management issues. There is definitely a trend with respect to lawyers at larger firms who are serving this dedicated resource role. We also have a larger team of lawyers and technologists who work collaboratively to efficiently manage the e-discovery process in large and small matters. I think it is a trend that makes sense. E-discovery represents a significant cost to our clients; therefore, tackling it with defensible strategies and people who understand the complications and technical issues that come with this process gives the client more reassurance that their e-discovery effort is being handled in the most appropriate and cost-effective way. We employ within our team lower billable rate discovery attorneys who do the day-to-day database and review management and analysis of data, to avoid charging clients the rates of our normal associates and partners to do some of that work. These lawyers and technologists are specially trained to make maximum use of the tools available and to focus the volumes down to the key documents that need to be reviewed by associates and partners on the case.

In an effort to capitalize on the exponential growth in e-discovery, some non-law firm companies are offering to handle the collection, hosting, review, and production of electronically stored information and provide the result to the outside counsel. As outside counsel, we are required to oversee this process in order to properly represent to the court what has been done and to ensure we identify the key documents we need for depositions and trial; therefore, we prefer to manage the e-discovery process in-house in order to maintain the consistency and quality of work that we expect. We want to ensure that the work gets done, and that it is done with accuracy and defensibility in litigation, or in response to government subpoenas.

Main e-Discovery Rules and Regulations

Most of the rules that govern e-discovery come from amendments to the Federal Rules of Civil Procedure, which were adopted in 2006, to address the reality that the discovery of "documents" also includes electronically stored information (ESI). The amendments modified existing rules related to discovery to include a discussion of ESI. The rules contemplate parties discussing e-discovery issues early in the case and set forth a framework for such issues as the format of production, scope of discovery, identification of sources that are not reasonably accessible, and proportionality. The key rules that affect e-discovery are Rules 1, 26, 33, 34, and 37.

There is also a body of case law in this area—largely in the federal courts, but also in state courts. The case law came before the Federal Rules were amended, but it has continued to develop and evolve since those amendments. States have addressed e-discovery through adoption of their own rules and case law; some have adopted rules similar to the federal rules, while others have gone on their own path. For example, some state rules have required greater front-end disclosure of documents while others have not adopted the Federal Rule's requirement that parties meet and confer to discuss these issues. There also is a body of local rules within the state and federal courts that individual districts, courts, or judges have put in place to establish protocols and guidelines related to e-discovery. A recent example of this is the Seventh Circuit's Electronic Discovery Pilot Program, which was initiated in May of 2009 as a multi-year, phased process to develop procedures to help manage e-discovery issues in a manner that reduces the burdens and costs while ensuring fairness to all parties—a tall order.

Consequently, we have a patchwork system of rules with regard to e-discovery. There is certainly not one uniform source for regulating the e-discovery process; the rules in this area come from lots of different places—state courts, federal courts, local standing orders, and so on. Much of the most detailed guidance comes through the evolving case law—case law that is very fact specific. These issues are usually decided by federal district courts and magistrate judges and are rarely in a procedural posture that allows for an appeal. Therefore, there is little appellate guidance on many of these issues. This area of the law is still developing, and different governing bodies are weighing in at different times and sometimes with different guidance.

Looking ahead, I see a push toward additional modifications to the federal rules to provide more guidance in the preservation area, as well as continued movement toward developing standard e-discovery guideposts. These changes are needed largely because of the severe consequences and sanctions that have been issued by courts in this area—especially with regard to preservation of ESI. E-discovery sanctions and costs have been increasing every year as the volume, burdens, and complications of managing electronic data continue to increase. Despite some sales pitches to the contrary, there is still no magic bullet solution to the complicated problem of managing, preserving, reviewing, analyzing, and producing ESI in litigation or regulatory matters.

Consequently, there is definitely an effort to try to bring some uniformity into how these processes are handled, reduce the burdens, and to give reliable and consistent guidance. Think tanks like the Sedona Conference have been publishing guidance and best practices recommendations even before the rules were amended and will continue to serve as useful resources to practitioners. Additionally, there is a movement for more formal modifications to the e-discovery rules, including narrowing the definition of "relevance," adding an intent standard for when sanctions may be imposed, and having increased judicial involvement. Groups such as The American College of Trial Lawyers Task Force of Discovery and the Institute for the Advancement of the American Legal System are pushing for modifications to the rules related to e-discovery. Other groups disagree that changes to the rules are required, and instead, think that the case law is filling in any gaps in the rules and that the current landscape is sufficient. In May of 2010, thought leaders convened at Duke University for the 2010 Conference on Civil Litigation to discuss some of these potential changes and to analyze the landscape that has evolved after the 2006 amendments to the Federal Rules. This meeting was sponsored by the Judicial Conference Advisory Committee on Civil Rules and involved a wide range of participants. This meeting should result in some concrete recommendations and proposals in the future.

The current landscape gives little comfort to clients having to make complex decisions relating to the management of ESI—especially in the area of preservation. However, it is difficult to say if any rule changes will occur in the near future or if some of these issues will be resolved through case law or other methods. One of the problems with respect to e-discovery is that the technology is constantly evolving and every case is different; therefore, as soon as you have a rule that addresses how to handle something like e-mail, an issue involving cloud computing pops up. As a result, the rule-makers in this area have tried to develop standards that are technology neutral and that address issues as they come forward. E-discovery law must be able to constantly evolve and adapt, based on new realities. I predict we will all continue to struggle with these issues for years to come.

Enforcing the Rules: e-Discovery Litigation

The e-discovery rules usually come into play in the court system; the courts are enforcing penalties for failure to properly preserve or identify relevant information and produce it in litigation. There is no single regulatory body that oversees e-discovery. Unfortunately, problems in this area are always based on an after the fact evaluation of what you have done. Many e-discovery-related decisions – such as what to preserve and for how long - may occur before a lawsuit is filed. Accordingly, you cannot simply go to a court and ask a judge if you are doing e-discovery in the right way, which is one of the issues that makes this a complicated area.

A large number of cases have been decided addressing e-discovery issues, including preservation, collection, production, and spoliation of ESI. Statistics show that there was the equivalent of one e-discovery decision for every business day of 2009. Again, these decisions are highly fact-specific, and you must piece all of them together to see which ones are closely related to the facts in your case. Among the more recent opinions in this area getting attention is an opinion by Judge Shira A. Scheindlin of the Southern District of New York that revisited some issues addressed in her earlier precedent-setting case law regarding e-discovery—the series of opinions decided in 2003-2004 in the *Zubulake* case: Zubulake v. UBS Warburg, 217 F.R.D. 309 (S.D.N.Y. 2003); Zubulake v. UBS Warburg, 220 F.R.D. 212 (S.D.N.Y. 2003); and Zubulake v. UBS Warburg, 2004 WL 1620866 (S.D.N.Y. July 20, 2004). The *Zubulake* opinions predate the amendments to the Federal Rules and continue to be some of the most frequently cited cases for issues such as when the duty to preserve ESI is triggered.

Judge Schiendlin's recent opinion—subtitled "Zubulake Revisited"—involved sanctions against thirteen different plaintiffs for a wide array of negligent and grossly negligent e-discovery errors, including the failure to issue a written legal hold. Pension Comm. of Univ. of Montreal Pension Plan v. Bank of Am. Secs. LLC, 2010 WL 184312 (S.D.N.Y. Jan. 15, 2010) (Amended Order). The issues were so fact-intensive that it took over eighty pages to describe the various failures of the plaintiffs' efforts to preserve, identify, collect, and produce ESI. The opinion criticizes some of the parties for relying on individual custodians to preserve and/or collect relevant electronically stored documents. This issue of how much responsibility can be placed on individual users for preservation and collection continues to evolve and is an area that is worthy of close attention given the costs and risks involved in the e-discovery process. The opinion is notable because plaintiffs were sanctioned, in some instances, for being negligent or sloppy in their e-discovery efforts, but not blatantly trying to delete or destroy information. This case also demonstrates the importance of documenting the e-discovery processes, involving appropriate parties in the strategy and execution, and understanding the pitfalls that may await an unsuspecting litigant.

Judge Scheindlin's opinion is just one of many significant opinions decided so far this year and no doubt the "Case Law Update" webcasts available will continue to overflow with content. Due to the incredibly fact-specific nature of e-discovery issues, lawyers in this area must stay current and read the cases as they come down to ensure they are crafting reasonable solutions and strategies that address these concerns.

Components of an e-Discovery Strategy

The most important aspect of any e-discovery strategy is to tailor it to the issues involved in the specific matter for which e-discovery is being sought. Therefore, it is important to look at the particular reason that the e-discovery is being requested, the nature of the controversy, the parties involved, and the relevant deadlines. A governmental inquiry is different from litigation, and within litigation, there are different types of litigation that implicate different types of data and approaches. For example, a bet-the-company patent infringement lawsuit involving software design may require production of proprietary source code to an escrow agent to ensure its authentication and to prevent it from being accessible to competitors; an insurance coverage case may require the export of policy-specific claim information from a proprietary centralized database, but may not require sifting through five years worth of e-mails; and a sexual harassment lawsuit may focus on e-mails and instant messages for a targeted period, but not require the review of other data sources. Therefore, it is vital not to have a "one size fits all" standard strategy, but to customize the e-discovery strategy based on the amount in controversy; the nature of the claims; the nature of the client's own data systems; and the nature of the opposing party in litigation. If two large companies are litigating against each other, the strategy is a little different than if you are the only party with data, or you are the party with the largest volume of data. Examples of cases where one party may not have much data to collect or produce are cases involving a single individual or class of individuals against a corporation. The individuals may only have one home computer to search, if at all, and the corporation may have fifteen data centers and 150 individual global data custodians. You have a bit more room for compromise and negotiation when both parties are dealing with these burdens than when it is a one-sided affair.

It is always important to do a detailed factual investigation in the e-discovery process. It is important to incorporate the e-discovery strategy with the overall case strategy. For example, when you are interviewing the key data custodians regarding the underlying facts, you should also be inquiring about potential data sources and gather information about the individual custodian's storage habits. You should also interview appropriate personnel from the client's IT department to make sure you understand the systems and sources that may be relevant to your matter. You will want to know if there are any systems in place that could cause the loss of relevant data and whether there are some sources that need extra steps to preserve. Through your investigation, you should be able to identify sources that are readily accessible and highly relevant, and sources that are more tangential and/or less accessible. For example, you may identify disaster recovery tapes containing e-mail from the relevant time period. You should assess whether this is the only source for such e-mail or if there is another more accessible source. To the extent relevant data may reside on legacy systems or other less accessible media, you should gain an understanding of the burdens and costs involved in accessing such data, assess whether the data is available from more readily accessible sources, determine if the data is likely to be duplicative or cumulative, and consider seeking cost-sharing if the data is being requested by the opposing party. Another strategic consideration to handling such sources is to seek staged discovery starting with the more readily accessible sources and reserving the production of more tangential or less accessible sources only if the readily accessible sources prove insufficient.

Another key part of any effective e-discovery strategy is to identify areas of agreement with opposing counsel (or the government), such as scope limitations, production format, and confidentiality and non-waiver agreements. It is important to identify sources that the parties will not produce because they are not reasonably accessible, or because of undue cost or burden. You should also seek to focus the timeframe for discovery, to identify key custodians and sources for production, and to discuss specific search and retrieval strategies, and whether or not they are going to be appropriate in any given case. For example, can you agree to limit your searches and production to certain file types such as e-mails and standard user-generated data? Can you rely on search terms or sampling to test terms?

Due to the large volumes of ESI involved in many matters, it is important to address issues related to privilege. Federal Rule of Evidence 502 was enacted to avoid the harsh waiver of privilege that can occur through the inadvertent production of privileged documents. It was also intended to help reduce some of the highest costs associated with e-discovery—manual review of documents for privilege. You should consider entering into an agreement with opposing counsel under Rule 502 as a protection against waiver, but you should carefully weigh the consequences of relying on Rule 502 in lieu of a manual review. For maximum protection, you should seek to have any non-waiver agreement entered by the Court as an Order. You should also negotiate with opposing counsel (or the government) regarding whether or not you have to log all privileged documents after the filing of a lawsuit, and how you are going to handle logging in terms of e-mail strings. For example, will you treat an entire string as one document and enter it on the log once or will you log each message in the string separately? The latter option is more time consuming and expensive.

My general rule of thumb for an e-discovery strategy is simply to have one, and to plan as early as possible to deal with these issues. You need to seek agreement with the other side at the outset and be very candid about what you are doing. This is an area where if you are not openly negotiating and discussing these issues as the rules require, you could wind up in a situation where you are going to incur unnecessary costs and possibly sanctions for not having addressed some of these issues early on. For example, in the *Pension Committee* decision, Judge Scheindlin sanctioned some plaintiffs, in part, for failing to collect from *all* custodians who may have had anything to do with the litigation—even only a passing involvement. If the parties had negotiated the custodians for collection and production, this would not have been an issue. Similarly, if you unilaterally select search terms or date ranges for collection, and the other side disagrees with your selection, you may be required to go back, recollect, and re-review additional documents, causing delays and increased costs in duplication of effort.

Key Players in the e-Discovery Strategy

The key players in an e-discovery strategy are the case team, client, e-discovery liaisons, and in some instances, technologists or experts. The key players will vary. In my firm, we have dedicated resources to assist in developing the e-discovery strategy including myself and other members of the Electronic Discovery and Data Management Team. We can assist in decisions and negotiations relating to scope of discovery, format of production, identification of sources that are not readily accessible, as well as which tools to use for collection, review, and production. We also work to develop an appropriate strategy for review and for the identification of key documents for use at depositions and trial. Other participants should include appropriate representatives from the client, including the relevant custodians of the electronic data. If you are doing e-discovery in response to a regulatory/governmental inquiry, you should consult the government about the strategy in order to get an idea of the scope of the production and the focus of the inquiry, and to find areas for agreement. You should also make sure you understand any production format requirements.

Certainly, the opposing party should be involved in informing your strategy. You want to be reasonable in your approach and to understand the scope of discovery sought by the other side and the reasons for such requests. For example, if they are seeking all e-mails for a two-year period in order to prove that the company knew a merger was going to occur, you may be able to stipulate to that fact and reduce the date range for e-discovery. You need to give the other party what they need, but you also need to balance the costs and burdens of e-discovery with the desire to get to the relevant documents. You also want to make sure they produce what you need. Consider your own need for documents from the other side when deciding on the scope you are willing to use. Understanding the facts and issues of the case will help you with this decision.

Finally, in many cases you should consult with appropriate technologists or experts to make sure your strategy involves proper methods for collection and production. Additionally, some cases may warrant engaging a forensics expert to delve into complex issues related to restoring or identifying deleted data, access to secure files, or tracking of access to documents or data. Some cases where this may be necessary are cases alleging theft of trade secrets, corporate espionage, fraud, or similar cases.

e-Discovery Issues in Litigation

As an e-discovery attorney, I would argue that e-discovery is critical throughout the lifecycle of the case. Certainly early on in the case, e-discovery issues must be addressed to ensure relevant electronically stored information (ESI) is preserved to avoid the risk of sanctions or losing the information that you need to defend or bring your lawsuit. Therefore, very early case assessment, including assessing what data is available and making sure it gets preserved, is crucial. ESI may be preserved in a number of ways including "preservation in place" or by forensically copying over relevant ESI to a designated location for preservation. Different cases may require different approaches.

Also, whether you are a plaintiff or a defendant in litigation, or just auditing compliance for an internal or governmental investigation, it is important to use the tools and technology that are available to do an early case assessment of key documents. Doing this type of assessment at the outset of a case can help to save costs, and formulate an overall strategy for whether you want to bring a lawsuit or settle early on because you realize that the claim that is being made is valid. There is no sense in sifting through loads of data and going all the way down the path of full-blown litigation if you can quickly analyze your key data and find the truth of the matter—i.e., you cannot defend against the claim and a quick settlement is more cost-effective than incurring the costs to mount a defense.

Once a case is filed, e-discovery is an important part of the early negotiations with the other side, given its significant costs. In fact, if the e-discovery process is not incorporated into the overall strategy, the costs of the process can quickly overcome the value of the actual underlying lawsuit. Therefore, it is very important to think about these issues before you agree to include certain search terms and custodian lists. You need to be able to test your strategy to see what is going to be involved in the e-discovery process. For example, if you agree to produce all e-mails that hit on a certain list of terms without testing the utility of these terms, you could be committing to a costly undertaking without inquiring into the burdens and likelihood of relevancy.

Electronic discovery continues to be relevant once you get into depositions, summary judgment, and other briefing. Getting a handle on the e-mails and documents that an individual has generated during any specific period of time, and preparing them to talk about those documents in a deposition or to cross-examine another witness on those topics is a crucial part of getting to the underlying facts of any case. Understanding the ESI in a case also is key at trial and can help undercut or support a witnesses' testimony. Juries have come to expect a "smoking gun" e-mail—i.e., an e-mail that proves one side is right or wrong, and they expect to see electronic documents presented as evidence in cases ranging from business disputes to divorce actions. Therefore, e-discovery plays an important role throughout the lifecycle of the litigation.

Attorney-Client Privilege in e-Discovery and Litigation

One of the reasons why the cost of e-discovery is so expensive is that it includes the element of protecting the attorney-client privilege. If documents and communications are produced that are protected by the attorney-client privilege or attorney work-product protections, there is a risk that these protections will be waived and that confidential and protected information will be disclosed. Accordingly, to avoid such disclosures, you have to rely on a combination of technology and human beings to identify and log potentially privileged information. This may require the manual page by page review of large volumes of ESI—at significant cost.

There also are non-privileged reasons for wanting to review documents before you produce them, including reviewing documents for responsiveness, identifying confidential documents, and identifying key documents for use in depositions and trial. Regardless of the reasons for the manual review, the greatest cost of anything related to e-discovery tends to be the manual review by attorneys of large volumes of documents. In many cases, the privilege review can be the most burdensome aspect of the review because of volume as well as because of the need to use appropriately qualified attorneys to conduct such reviews. Therefore, evaluating the risk of waiving privilege, and the pros and cons of whether or not you should do a manual privilege review or rely on technology to pre-screen documents, certainly affects the overall litigation strategy.

There are certain cases where attorney-client privilege is not an issue, depending on the nature of the client's business or the source of the ESI for production. For example, the relevant custodians may not communicate with counsel or deal with legal issues and are thus less likely to have potentially privileged data in their possession. Similarly, data from certain systems may be less likely to contain privileged communications or work product, such as raw data from a financial reporting database. Such sources may not require review for potentially privileged information. Conversely, a detailed privilege review can be one of the largest issues in the case. For example, if you have two corporations arguing over a deal that has gone wrong, and there are large volumes of internal lawyers involved on both sides plus outside litigation counsel, it can be a very difficult endeavor to parse out the privileged communications from the non-privileged communications.

Integrating the e-Discovery Process into the Litigation Strategy

Our firm integrates the e-discovery process into the litigation strategy by incorporating the e-discovery team with the case team early in the litigation. Both teams work together and in conjunction with the client to develop strategies, recommend appropriate tools, and to handle e-discovery issues with opposing counsel. Throughout the stages of litigation, even preparing for depositions and trial, it is important to have an integrated team that can handle both the substantive parts of the case and the e-discovery issues.

The Role of Technology in the e-Discovery Strategy

Technology plays a huge role throughout the cycle of e-discovery. Certainly, we have seen a trend by corporations that are investing in technology on the front end to help them preserve, identify, and collect electronic information. Such technology includes e-mail archiving systems and other types of what I would call "left of the continuum" tools on to the Electronic Discovery Reference Model (EDRM). For example, many of our clients are investing in technology to assist them with search and retrieval of relevant information during the early case assessment stage, including e-mails or other user-generated data that may help them better assess the potential strengths and weaknesses of their claims or defenses. Technology also comes into play once you are at the stage where you need to begin to identify and collect information for actual litigation. Tools are used for collecting, processing, culling, analyzing, and reviewing ESI and to manage the process effectively and efficiently. Technology can be used to help sift through very large volumes of information, and focus in on the truly relevant information. Technology can also be used to develop cost-effective strategies for identifying, reviewing, and producing relevant ESI including concept searching, near-dupe analysis, and shared Web-based repositories that promote collaboration with clients, experts, and in some cases, other parties.

This area continues to change from year to year; and the tools are trying to catch up to the problem. You could not possibly do e-discovery without the tools that currently exist to help you with searching, processing, reviewing, and producing documents. Tools help to remove systems files, eliminate duplicates, and spot gaps in productions or collections. There are also many analytical tools that help reduce the need for relying on human beings to manually make sense of a large volume of information. Technology is essential once you continue through the process of preparing for depositions by identifying key documents related to key custodians. Technology is also used to help with the presentation and display of documents once you get to trial.

The specific individuals involved with respect to the use of e-discovery technology will vary from case to case—for example, you may need a forensic image of a hard drive, or you may need forensic experts to determine the life cycle of a particular document. You may also need technologists and litigation support professionals to assist in selecting appropriate tools and production formats. If there are issues of spoliation, you may need to engage experts to perform an analysis of those issues and whether or not data was improperly destroyed or deleted. However, given the cost of a truly forensic analysis of data, the use of a particular technology will depend on the nature of the claim. I find that forensic analysis is more commonly used in cases involving trade secrets or corporate raiding claims, or where there is any sort of allegation of fraud. In other cases, a forensic analysis of a computer or other data sources is not necessary; you may just need an e-discovery consultant to assist with doing a data collection in a forensically sound way. I definitely think that such a consultant can be a very good resource—especially when clients do not have the internal capacity or experience to do a proper collection, document the process, and create the necessary chain of custody.

Protecting Electronic Information

We advise our clients to have strong confidentiality agreements in place, and where possible, to get them in the form of a protective order with the court in order to protect against both the potential waiver of privilege and the handling of competitively sensitive information. Such a protective order also may address issues of privacy such as cases where the ESI may contain personal data or customer data.

It is also important to consider how to enforce those agreements with the other side in a way that makes sense. The volume of information in these cases can make it difficult to enforce confidentiality agreements—and courts are not necessarily friendly to you assigning a confidentiality designation to all of the documents that you produce. That gets back to the issue of whether you should manually review everything in order to make that confidentiality determination. Alternatively, you can put some protocols in place that have a default confidentiality designation, and when something is identified for filing or use in the case, you can then revisit that document to determine how it should be handled. Therefore, this is a case specific inquiry, but in any case, the baseline level of protection would be to have an appropriate protective order in place.

The Evolution of Electronic Records Management Systems

The use of electronic records management systems comes up in different contexts in the e-discovery process. It is first used in the true records management context on the left side of the continuum, including e-mail and record archiving systems; systems that allow you to categorize documents based on their retention period; and systems that give you the ability to search across various sources for responsive and relevant information. Records management systems are used once you have collected certain records and are engaged in putting them in a litigation-type database.

Typically, when you use the phrase "electronic management system" you are referring to the client's day-to-day system for managing data before litigation arises. Such systems are evolving to add components that specifically address and acknowledge e-discovery problems, including features that give you the ability to automate and track litigation holds and isolate data subject to the holds; the ability to locate that data wherever it may reside, including local computers or network servers; and a system for releasing those holds whenever the appropriate time arises.

Simply put, I am seeing a trend where the makers of electronic records management systems are understanding that there needs to be an e-discovery component to their systems, and there is a great deal of competition in that space, given the value that such technology can bring to the client. There are currently many different companies, products, and services offering some variation of an e-discovery component, and they are not all created equal. Therefore, the selection of an electronic records management system really depends on the needs of the client and their business. I definitely see the technology in this space trying to capture some of the things that are farther on the right side of the spectrum, including having methods for collection and review of documents, and transferring the documents from one platform to another under the same umbrella. There is a trend to try to consolidate these various steps in the e-discovery process under one technology suite, and the vendors seem to be in stiff competition to develop the system that everyone is going to want to use to solve all of their problems.

Disclosure Rules for e-Discovery

If you are involved in a case in federal court, Federal Rule of Civil Procedure 26(a) requires the parties to make certain initial disclosures including a description by category and location of documents and ESI and the identification of individuals likely to have discoverable information. The federal rules also contemplate that the parties will meet and confer to discuss scope, sources of ESI, and production formats.

Disclosures with respect to e-discovery can come up in other contexts, such as when you are served with a subpoena from a governmental regulatory body or in the criminal context. Consequently, the disclosure rules are simply part of the discovery process in general; therefore, I believe that the amendments to the rules were meant to clarify that when you are discovering information in litigation, it should also include the disclosure of relevant electronically stored information.

Using Attorney-Client Privilege to Protect Electronic Information

The use of attorney-client privilege to protect electronic information is a problem that we have not solved completely. We try to rely on all types of search terms to identify potentially privileged documents, although in some cases, that is not always a perfect solution, and there are issues with that process as well. This is a significant area for generating costs and for risk, because the disclosure of privileged communication is a serious issue—and that is why protections exist to protect these types of communications. However, given the increase in the volume of e-discovery data and the burdens that come with this process, there is certainly an increased risk that those types of communications will be produced. This is why I recommend that clients have a protective order in place to claw back those documents if they are inadvertently produced, and to create some agreements, where possible, about how these types of issues are going to be handled before a dispute arises.

I have found that it is useful to rely on Rule 502 to have some protections in place in the event that you have an inadvertent disclosure. The original purpose of the rule was to reduce some of the costs of discovery and risks by not requiring a manual review; you could essentially take some reasonable steps to filter out privileged information, and then produce everything else. However, there is still a risk of disclosing privileged information if you do not take all of the necessary steps and simply rely on the quick peek guidelines. As an initial matter, once that information is produced, you cannot "un-ring the bell." Secondly, some courts have still found waiver where the steps taken to avoid production were deemed not reasonably sufficient. Even in cases where a complete manual review is performed, having a Rule 502 agreement is advisable given the high risk of human error in large-volume reviews.

Another debate regarding Rule 502 is the issue of whether or not it really protects you from intentional disclosure; in other words, can you really just get a protective order issued pursuant to the rule, release all of your documents, rely on Rule 502 to claw back anything that ends up emerging from the pile, and then claim non-waiver? Although I think that is what Rule 502 is intended to do, there is some ambiguity inherent in the rule that has resulted in courts still requiring reasonable efforts to avoid the production of documents. Consequently, it has been my recommendation with respect to the language of the protective order to be very clear about what steps you are taking to avoid disclosure. If you are just relying on the quick peek component, you need to be very clear about that, and make sure that you include specific language to avoid any waiver. You should make sure there is no ambiguity before the court enters such an order.

Challenges in Obtaining Electronic Information

The physical challenges of identifying and collecting ESI from various sources can add additional burdens compared to the hard copy days. Additionally, individual custodians and clients may be more reluctant to produce ESI due to the horror stories of personal or embarrassing e-mails being divulged. Our discovery system in the U.S. often causes some level of discomfort for people who are not used to it; it can be difficult to accept the need to produce to a competitor documents that contain sensitive information about your business. Clients are often reluctant to reveal and disclose such documents.

Despite advances in technology, there are still risks associated with producing ESI, including the production of non-responsive documents or disclosure of privileged information. There is no magic way to find what is relevant in all cases. You can rely on search strategies and e-mail domains, but there will often be some irrelevant and personal information in the mix. Therefore, it is often a cost-benefit analysis as to whether or not you invest the time and energy to make sure that such information gets weeded out through a manual review process, or whether you risk disclosing it in order to save costs by not having to manually review those documents. You can certainly put in place a protective order or some procedure for protecting that type of information to make sure it does not make its way into other hands. However, you may still need to produce sensitive documents to the other party who, in many cases, can be your competitor—the very person you would not want knowing your trade secret information or business strategies. It is surprising to many clients that they actually have to turn over such documents to the other side in some cases.

Looking to the Future

I think that e-discovery technology will continue to evolve, and we will continue to see the types of consolidation that we have seen in this space as vendors and service providers seek to find solutions that will help us to manage the incredible volume of information being generated. I think the case law in this area will continue to evolve as well, in order to address changing technologies. For example, now that people better understand the e-discovery dangers with respect to e-mail and instant messaging and Web 2.0 technology use has increased, I can see the rules and the case law changing to address these emerging technologies in the way we communicate and store data. I also think we are going to have to address some of the complications associated with cloud computing and other sources that are not in the traditional line of stored data that the client can control and access because it is stored out "in the cloud" by third party providers. The intermingling of personal and business data on iPhones and similar devices will also pose problems.

Going forward, I think the case law and court rules will continue to evolve to try to reach some sort of meaningful balance between the cost and burdens of e-discovery, and the need to obtain relevant information. Even as vendors try to find a technological solution to these issues, the courts are realizing the cost and burden that e-discovery is creating; in some cases, people are reaching settlements to avoid the potential cost of e-discovery. Fortunately, there are efforts underway to reform this area and make sure that it is meeting the needs of litigants.

I do not know if the case law in this area will continue to expect and require that corporations invest in the kind of technology that allows them to retrieve information readily, or if it will strike a balance and take into consideration the facts and proportionality requirements of a particular case. Currently, this practice area can be challenging, because there is a lack of consistent guidance in many areas and so many determinations are fact-driven.

Final Thoughts

I would advise new attorneys that if you feel that you did not go to law school to work with computers and databases, then you might want to rethink being a litigator in the modern era, because you really cannot avoid dealing with e-discovery. If you are a more senior litigator who thinks that e-discovery cannot substantively affect your case, you might also want to reconsider that notion, because as the case law in this area has proved, claims can be dismissed if e-discovery is handled incorrectly. Therefore, I think it is advisable to get informed about these issues and, where appropriate, work with someone who lives and breathes e-discovery to make sure you are adequately addressing these issues throughout the life cycle of the litigation. It is important to avoid unnecessary costs and burdens on both sides while making sure that relevant information is identified and used and get to the merits of the case without being sidetracked by some of these issues.

Key Takeaways

- To successfully manage e-discovery, you must understand the sources of ESI, the specific claims and facts at issue, and develop an appropriate plan of action in light of these issues.
- You must seek agreement through collaboration with opposing counsel in order to avoid pitfalls, focus the e-discovery issues, and avoid potentially side-tracking the case into a spiral of e-discovery disputes.
- Where agreement is not possible, you must have a detailed and reasonable plan to seek relief from the court.

- You need to be aware of the pros and cons of relying on Rule 502 regarding inadvertent disclosures in e-discovery, and make sure that you have an agreement in place that addresses the various ways your reliance on that rule could come back to be an issue.
- Get informed about these issues and work with e-discovery experts where appropriate to make sure you are adequately addressing e-discovery issues throughout the life cycle of the litigation.

Alison A. Grounds is an of counsel in the Complex Litigation and Intellectual Property practice groups of Troutman Sanders LLP. Ms. Grounds is the co-founder and co-leader of the firm's Electronic Discovery and Data Management Team. Ms. Grounds is experienced in litigating various complex commercial and business disputes related to contractual rights, fraud, business torts, products liability, trademarks, copyrights, domain names, technology, false advertising, trade secrets, and unfair competition.

Ms. Grounds is based in Atlanta and works with all of the firm's offices and attorneys on e-discovery issues. She counsels clients regarding litigation readiness and data management, serves as national coordinating discovery counsel to clients, designs cost-effective and case-specific strategies for handling e-discovery in litigation and internal/governmental investigation, and represents clients in legal disputes related to e-discovery during litigation. Ms. Grounds is also a member of The Sedona Conference Working Group on Electronic Document Retention and Production (WG1) and DRI's Electronic Discovery Committee. Ms. Grounds graduated with honors from the University of North Carolina at Chapel Hill School of Law.

New Trends in e-Discovery Compliance and Enforcement

Christopher G. Buenik

Partner

Bollinger, Ruberry & Garvey

ASPATORE

Key Federal e-Discovery Rules

Among the most important federal e-discovery rules are Federal Rule of Civil Procedure (FRCP) 26(a)(1)(A)(ii) (specifies electronically stored information (ESI) must be produced without a request for any relevant document including any e-mail or data), FRCP 16(c)(2)(G) (parties shall identify ESI), 26(b)(2)(B) (a party need not disclose ESI from sources not reasonably accessible because of undue burden or cost), 26(b)(5)(B) (if inadvertently disclose privileged information, may request it be returned), 26(f)(3) (requires parties to discuss and include in a plan "any issues about disclosure or discovery of electronically stored information including the form or forms in which it should be produced"), 26(g)(1) (requires certification of accuracy by attorney), 34(b)(2)(E) (a party must disclose ESI in the form it is kept in the usual course of business or must organize and label the ESI to correspond to the request), 34(a)(1)(A) (a party may request a copy of all ESI that can be obtained from any medium either directly or after translation into a reasonably useable form), 34(b)(2)(D) (the responding party may object to the form in which the data is requested. If there was not a form specified in the disclosure request, the responding party must state the form or forms it intends to use), 34(b)(2)(E)(ii) (if a production form is not specified in the request, a party must disclose it in the form it is kept in the usual course of business or in a reasonably useable form), 37(e) (absent exceptional circumstances, a court may not sanction a party for failing to provide ESI lost as a result of routine, good-faith operation of the information system), 45(a)(C) (a subpoena may specify the form or forms in which electronically stored information is to be produced), and 45(d)(1)(A)-(D) (procedures for producing electronically stored information via subpoena). Generally, FRCP 26-34, 37, and 45 are the rules that most often apply to e-discovery.

Typically, e-mails are most often sought under these rules, as they are the most common source of valuable electronic information possessed by litigants. Metadata is also often desired because it provides a trail of highly relevant information regarding the who, what, and when of ESI.

Significant Cases in e-Discovery

The landmark decisions of Zubulake vs. UBS Warburg, 220 F.R.D.212 (S.D.N.Y. 2003) (Zubulake IV) and Zubulake v. UBS Warburg, 2004 WL

1620866 (S.D.N.Y July 20, 2004) (Zubulake V), were precedential in that they were decided prior to the 2006 amendments to the FRCP and imposed sanctions for failing to preserve ESI. The court ruled that a litigant should have "reasonably anticipated" that it had a responsibility to preserve electronic data in a wide area network prior to the lawsuit being filed and the failure to do so warranted an adverse inference instruction against the defendant. Essentially, these cases put the legal community on notice of the requirement to institute a litigation hold on e-discovery data, and the need for key employees to engage in e-mail archiving and effective destruction and retention policies. Although Rule 37(e) restricted the consequences of a party's failure to preserve ESI if the data was "lost as a result of the routine, good-faith operation of an electronic information system," a party is not necessarily immune from court imposed sanctions or a spoliation of evidence claim if the party knew or should have known of a potential claim and failed to suspend its routine destruction of potentially relevant data. FED. R. CIV. P. 26(b)(2), Committee Comment, 2006 Amendment. For instance, in *Keithley v. The Home Store.com Inc.*, the defendant's neglect in maintaining a litigation hold lead to the destruction of ESI and the imposition of an adverse inference instruction despite the lack of any "bad faith." Keithley v. The Home Store.com Inc., 2008 WL 3833384 (N.D. Cal. Aug. 12, 2008). Moreover, in Bray & Gillespie Mgmt. LLC v. Lexington Ins. Co., 2010 WL 55595 (M.D. Fla. Jan. 5, 2010), the court found that the plaintiffs' failure to consult with their software provider in order to preserve relevant evidence necessitated the dismissal of the claims arising from or related to the documents and ordered the plaintiffs to pay the defendant $75,000 in expenses and costs.

Also groundbreaking was Qualcomm Inc. vs. Broadcom Corp., 2008 WL 66932 (S.D. Cal. Jan. 7, 2008), for the effect that electronic discovery can have on a party for its non-compliance with discovery rules. In *Qualcomm*, the plaintiff was found to have withheld thousands of e-mails and other electronic data. Because of its conduct, the court sanctioned Qualcomm by awarding the defendant all of its attorney's fees and costs, amounting to more than $8.5 million. Another key e-discovery case is *Auto* Club Family Ins. Co. v. Ahner, 2007 WL 2480322 (E.D. La. Aug. 29, 2007). In this case, the parties issued subpoenas to a non-party seeking the production of ESI. The respondent agreed to produce the requested information in hard copy form but sought a protective order to prevent the production of any ESI.

The court noted that the respondent did not make an evidentiary showing that the data sought was not reasonably accessible because of undue burden or cost. Moreover, the court stated it "will not automatically assume that an undue burden or expense may arise simply because electronic evidence is involved." Noting that ESI is typically accessible in today's world, the court ordered that the respondent produce the requested ESI, and unless otherwise shown, was required to assume the costs associated with said production.

Although the trend has been to produce all relevant ESI, the scope of the discovery request must be reasonably tailored to meet the goals of discovery. In Moore v. Abbott Lab., 2008 WL 4981400 (S.D. Ohio Nov. 19, 2008), the plaintiff filed an employment discrimination lawsuit and moved to compel the production of documents without any restriction in time, geographic area or type. The defendant objected by arguing that it had previously produced 14,000 pages of documents and that the additional request would be cost prohibitive. In ruling for the defendant, the court stated that the plaintiff's discovery requests were "extraordinarily overbroad" and that the "mere speculation about relevance" is not enough to order the production. Additionally, in Aguilar v. Immigration & Customs Enforcement Divis. of U.S. Dept. of Homeland Sec., 2008 WL 5062700 (S.D.N.Y. Nov. 21, 2008), the court found that the parties' failure to discuss the production of metadata at the FRCP 26(f) conference rendered the plaintiff's requests for metadata related to e-mails and back-up tapes untimely and too costly for the little benefit potentially gained.

New e-Discovery Regulation

The Seventh Circuit, which covers Illinois, developed an e-discovery pilot program, of which Phase One has recently concluded by implementing specific recommendations for how to regulate and deal with electronic discovery. *Seventh Circuit Electronic Discovery Pilot Program – Phase One*, http://www.7thcircuitbar.org/associations/1507/files/05-2010%20Phase%20One%20Report%20and%20Appendix%20with%20Bookmarks.pdf. The goal of the program was to "incentivize early and informal information exchange on commonly encountered issues relating to evidence preservation and discovery" and find ways to reduce e-discovery costs. The following recommendations were made: (1) encourage attorney cooperation; (2) apply proportional standard for requests and related responses; (3) meet and confer to identify relevant ESI, designate production format, and discuss disputes and obtain resolutions; (4) designate e-discovery liaisons to assist in resolving disputes; (5) limit the scope of the preservation request to reduce costs; and (6) become familiar with the Federal Rules of Civil Procedure, Advisory Committee Report on the 2006 Amendments and these principles. The need for such a program is largely a result of the inherent difficulties involved in dealing with e-discovery for litigants and its implementation into the legal community. These recommendations will serve as a beacon for the management of e-discovery and will serve as a procedural framework for the parties and lawyers for the foreseeable future.

Issues and Impacts of Federal and State e-Discovery Rules

Many state court jurisdictions are following the lead of the federal courts by implementing new rules and laws to regulate e-discovery, including California, New Jersey, Minnesota, Texas, Utah, Louisiana, Arizona, Montana, and Indiana. Like the 2006 Federal Amendments, the crux of these state laws is to effectively manage the rising burden and costs of e-discovery. Unfortunately, in state court proceedings, the litigants generally fail to recognize the relevancy of e-discovery and how to effectively identify, preserve, collect, process, and produce it. For example, Illinois state court law allows any party to request "any and all retrievable information in computer storage." Ill. Sup. Ct. R. 201(b). However, few litigants seek to obtain electronically stored data and there often is a lack of inquiry regarding the same. Although there are no Illinois state court decisions directly sanctioning a party for failing to preserve or produce electronically stored information, Illinois and many jurisdictions recognize a cause of action for spoliation of evidence. In Boyd v. Travelers Ins. Co., 166 Ill.2d 188, 195 (1995), the Illinois Supreme Court recognized the failure to preserve evidence can create a spoliation of evidence claim if the loss or destruction of the evidence caused the plaintiff to be unable to prove an otherwise valid underlining cause of action. *Id.* at 197. As shown above, federal courts are not reluctant to sanction a party for disobeying their e-discovery obligations. Sanctions have ranged from the imposition of costs and adverse inference instructions to barring claims and default judgments. In the near future, it is likely that many state courts will begin to impose similar sanctions.

Consequences for Not Disclosing e-Discovery Information

During the Rule 26(f) conference, an informal discovery plan should be developed to identify the relevant ESI and to implement a best practice guideline. Effective project management will ensure that the discovery process is efficient and effective. Maintaining data accountability is critical for the identification and production of the original data and a litigation hold will ensure that all relevant data is preserved. Without the proper planning and effective management, relevant ESI is more susceptible to being destroyed and sanctions are likely to follow.

The consequences of not preserving and producing ESI vary, depending upon the scope and nature of the discovery rule violation. Sanctions have included an adverse inference instruction, monetary sanction, default judgment, and claim preclusion. For example, in a recent case, a court entered a monetary sanction against a party and its counsel for failing to identify and produce all sources of ESI. *See*, *In re* A&M Florida Props. II LLC v. Am. Federated Title Corp., 2010 WL 1418861, (Bankr. S.D.N.Y. Apr. 7, 2010). In *A&M Florida*, the court stated that counsel had an obligation to not only request all relevant data but to also search for all sources of information. The court stated that counsel should have become acquainted with the client's retention policies and retention architecture in order to have a dialogue to unearth all relevant data. *Id.*

On the state level, reported discovery sanctions are rare. However, through the utilization of existing state discovery rules, a party can seek ESI or sanctions for the failure to produce the same. Examples of common state court sanctions for failing to produce ESI include barring a claim or defense and adverse inference instructions.

The Role of Attorney-Client Privilege in Protecting Electronic Evidence

The inadvertent production of attorney-client information is a mistake that can be minimized with the proper foresight. A clawback agreement is a mechanism by which litigants can proceed with the production of documents and information without fear of waiving a privilege. The standard clawback agreement is a contract between litigants that states that the inadvertent production of privileged information does not automatically constitute a waiver if the producer realizes the mistake in a reasonable amount of time and promptly requests the return of the information. Utilizing the recent amendments to the Federal Rules of Civil Procedure 16(b)(3)(B)(iv) in conjunction with 26(b)(5), a litigant can incorporate a clawback provision in a protective order to further insulate privileged information. *See* FED. R. CIV. P. 16(b)(3)(B)(iv) and FED. R. CIV. P. 26(b)(5). Although courts generally enforce clawback agreements, they should not be used as the first line of defense. The courts commonly reject blanket clawback agreements and they are not necessarily enforced in subsequent litigation. Despite few drawbacks, litigants are too often ignoring the benefits of clawback agreements. In Victor Stanley Inc. v. Creative Pipe Inc., 250 F.R.D. 251 (D. Md. 2008), the defendant was requested to produce voluminous ESI and smartly requested that a clawback agreement be entered. However, after obtaining an extension to conduct a privilege review, the defendant withdrew its pursuit of a clawback agreement and made its ESI production to the plaintiff. *Id.* at 255. The plaintiff soon identified that 165 privileged documents were produced and filed a motion seeking a ruling that the attorney-client and work-product privileges were waived. The court ruled that any privilege was waived by the defendant; however, had a clawback agreement been entered, the documents would have been protected. *Id.* at 267-268.

Even without a clawback agreement, Federal Rule of Evidence 502 sets forth a mechanism to protect the inadvertent disclosure of privileged documents under specific circumstances. Pursuant to Rule 502(b), an inadvertent disclosure does not operate as a waiver if: (1) the disclosure is inadvertent; (2) the holder of the privilege or protection took reasonable steps to prevent disclosure; and (3) the holder promptly took reasonable steps to rectify the error, including (if applicable) following FRCP 26(b)(5)(B). *See* FED. R. EVID. 502 and FED. R. CIV. P. 26(b)(5)(B). For example, in Coburn Group, LLC v. Whitecap Advisors LLC, 640 F. Supp. 2d 1032 (N.D. Ill. 2009), the defendant produced to its counsel hard drives containing 72,000 pages of documents. The lead defense counsel supervised the review of the documents and implemented a protocol for two experienced paralegals to follow over a five-week privilege review. *Id.* at 1039. After producing 40,000 pages of documents, it was discovered that sixteen pages of privileged information was inadvertently produced. The court found that the defendant produced the documents by mistake, took reasonable steps to prevent the disclosure, and took reasonable steps to rectify the error. The court further found that the plaintiff failed to show a substantial need for inadvertently produced materials to prepare its case and therefore the plaintiff was ordered to return the documents to the defendant. *Id.* at 1041. By taking reasonable steps to prevent an inadvertent disclosure of privileged information and addressing the error immediately, parties will have a strong argument to mitigate the potential damage.

Recent court decisions have clearly shown that in order to reap the advantages of Federal Rule of Evidence 502, clients should be counseled to develop policies and procedures related to the identification, storage, and destruction of ESI. Through effective project management, the response to an e-discovery request will be limited in scope and the retention of relevant data will be accomplished. An e-discovery plan is essential to doing business in the twenty-first century and it will reduce the overall costs associated with e-discovery.

The Impact of the Seventh Circuit Pilot Program Principles

Upon completion of Phase One of the program, a comprehensive survey was conducted among the thirteen judges of the U.S. District Court for the Northern District of Illinois as well as 133 attorneys who participated in the ninety-three cases that were subject to the program. A summary of the survey results are as follows: 43 percent of the attorneys indicated that the principles "increased" or "greatly increased" fairness in the discovery process; 38 percent of the attorneys found that the principles "increased" the ability to resolve e-discovery disputes without judicial intervention; 67 percent of the judges stated that the proportionality principle played a significant role in developing e-discovery plans; 84 percent of the judges found that the principles "increased" or "greatly increased" the level of cooperation among attorneys; 92 percent of judges indicated that the principles had a positive effect on the meaningful attempts by attorneys to resolve e-discovery disputes; and 100 percent of the judges found that the e-discovery liaison contributed to a more efficient discovery process. *Seventh Circuit Electronic Discovery Pilot Program – Report on Phase One*, http://www.7thcircuitbar.org/associations/1507/files/05-2010%20Phase %20One%20Report%20and%20Appendix%20with%20Bookmarks.pdf.

As evidenced by the results, the implementation of the Seventh Circuit Pilot Program Principles on a full-scale basis will likely lead to significant gains in educating the legal community on the importance of preparing for and managing e-discovery issues, as well as fostering cooperation between opposing counsel and reducing costs and resolving discovery disputes. The survey results will be further examined to modify the principles in areas that were not effective and to explore issues that were not adequately addressed.

Although results of the survey demonstrated that the attorneys were less enthusiastic about the effectiveness of the principles as compared to the judges, it is clear that the overarching principles of the pilot program will have a profound impact on how the everyday practitioner confronts e-discovery issues. Ultimately, the principles will lead to a reduction in the overall cost of e-discovery and promote fair dealing among litigants.

Preserving e-Discovery in Litigation

Preserving ESI is imperative from the moment that a party "reasonably anticipates litigation." The determination of when a party should reasonably anticipate litigation is not clearly defined with a bright-line rule. Accordingly, prudence demands that counsel immediately place a litigation hold to suspend the routine destruction of ESI. Additionally, counsel should identify the key personnel likely to have knowledge of relevant information and the computer system in order to identify, preserve, collect, process, review, and produce all relevant information. Employees should be directed to produce electronic copies of all relevant active files and the litigation hold should be monitored to ensure compliance. The failure to heed these directives can result in severe sanctions. For example, in Merck Eprova AG v. Gnosis S.P.A., 2010 WL 1631519 (S.D.N.Y. Apr. 20, 2010), the plaintiff sought sanctions against the defendant for failing to alter its document retention/destruction policy and neglecting to institute a litigation hold after receiving notice of the lawsuit. *Id.* at 1. The court stated that the failure to initiate a litigation hold constitutes gross negligence. *Id.* at 11. The court held that the defendant had notice of the lawsuit and it clearly took no steps to suspend the destruction of ESI. The court therefore granted the plaintiff's motion and entered sanctions against the defendant including the costs expended to acquire the documents and a $25,000 monetary fine to deter future misconduct. The court also reserved the right to impose an adverse inference instruction in the future. *Id.* at 12.

While the litigation hold is fundamental, it is equally important to develop a plan to respond to a request for ESI. It is becoming commonplace to create a separate repository for electronic information in order to maintain the authenticity of the information and substantiate the preservation and production of all relevant information. The creation of backup tapes of all electronic data is another method commonly used to protect against the accidental destruction of relevant information.

Electronic Management Systems

An electronic document management system is a computer program that indexes and stores company records. The paramount objectives in selecting an electronic document management system with respect to e-discovery are storage and retrieval capabilities. There are certainly different platforms that companies can utilize. For example, software programs such as CEBOS MQ1 and Oracle Content Management reduce the time and effort that lawyers need to spend on e-discovery through versatile yet user-friendly processes. By focusing on the processes of e-discovery—identification, preservation, collection, processing, review, and production—you will be in the best position to select a system to meet your e-discovery and business needs.

The Role of Experts in Managing e-Discovery Issues

Computer forensics has been defined as "the use of specialized techniques for recovery, authentication and analysis of electronic data when an investigation or litigation involves issues relating to reconstruction of computer usage, examination of residual data, authentication of data by technical analysis or explanation of technical features of data and computer usage. Computer forensics require specialized expertise that goes beyond normal data collection and preservation techniques available to end-users or system support personnel, and generally requires strict adherence to chain-of-custody protocols." *The Sedona Conference Glossary: E-Discovery & Digital Information Management* (Second Edition) Dec. 2007, *available at* http://www.thesedonaconference.org/. A computer forensic expert may be required to navigate the labyrinth of e-discovery, particularly in cases involving the deletion and retrieval of relevant information. In order to reduce costs, most litigants utilize a hybrid of outside consultants and in-house IT personnel to implement and execute an e-discovery plan. Depending upon the nature and value of the case, specialized computer forensic experts can be integral in identifying, restoring, and preserving deleted information. Simply put, e-discovery compliance is typically beyond the ken of many lawyers, and therefore they will often look to a specialist who has more experience in this area.

The occasional federal court litigator who is not familiar with the e-discovery juggernaut will be well served to seek outside consultation to assist in the e-discovery process. The first crucial step is to cease normal file deletion and institute a litigation hold in order to protect against a spoliation claim and court imposed sanctions. Thereafter, a computer forensic expert can be consulted to provide guidance on the necessary strategies to successfully prosecute or defend a lawsuit. Computer forensics is especially useful in measuring the quality of the e-discovery through statistical sampling. These methods are typically approved by courts and are instrumental in identifying key evidence, minimizing inadvertent disclosure of privileged information, and reducing long-term costs. In summary, a successful e-discovery strategy will encompass the use of computer forensics—whether your plan will include outside experts, in-house employees or a combination of both will depend upon the type and size of the litigation.

Successful Strategies

Clients and attorneys who do not properly disclose e-discovery information could face monetary fines, adverse inference instructions, and claim dismissal or preclusion. Consequently, each client and attorney should utilize and develop best practices to ensure that the client and attorney are complying with the e-discovery rules. A best practices protocol should include the implementation of a data retention/destruction policy, the initiation of a litigation hold, the formation of key personnel to respond to e-discovery (including an outside computer consultant), and the familiarization of the computer system and storage systems.

In terms of developing an effective e-discovery strategy, the key elements are education, training, and implementation. First and foremost, you need to educate your clients that in today's world, an e-discovery plan is an essential business practice. After a plan has been assembled and disseminated, periodic training to effectively execute the plan will prevent mistakes during critical moments. After a lawsuit has been filed, the attorney must continually work with the client to enforce the e-discovery plan and seek computer expert consultation as needed.

Looking to the Future

From a technological standpoint, advances in data storage, mapping, and searching for data will reduce the unnecessary production of irrelevant documents and related costs associated therein. Document management systems are an effective tool to control data efficiently and companies will likely seek to internalize e-discovery expenses by incorporating these different types of software as a formal business practice. Although cost savings are the primary objective of document management systems, ease of use and access to data and security are often as important to managing e-discovery. The incorporation of unofficial rules concerning how litigants preserve, identify, collect, process, and produce ESI will likely become a standardized practice in the e-discovery process. Learning the ins and outs of e-discovery now will likely prevent a future disaster.

In the future, virtually all documents and records will contain ESI. Therefore, the days of not requesting and producing e-discovery in litigated matters are vanishing. As a natural response, it is increasingly likely that people and corporations will attempt to insulate information such that it is not "reasonably accessible" to prevent disclosure and reduce costs. The result may create a tug of war between overly broad production requests and cost savings. Already, litigation strategies have been employed to make the costs of e-discovery so prohibitive that it discourages requests from "sources not reasonably accessible because of undue burden and cost." (e.g., Rodriguez-Torres v. Gov't Dev. Bank of Puerto Rico, 2010 WL 174156 (D.P.R. Jan. 20, 2010) holding that the $35,000 cost of producing ESI was "too high" in light of a $1.4 million prayer for relief). Consequently, cunning parties will seek data retention policies and document management systems that best serve their business and litigation interests.

Looking ahead, I believe that sampling software tools will be refined in order to verify the accuracy of the production of electronic discovery and advancements in computer software programs will greatly reduce costs. While there may always be some skepticism with respect to the quality of data that is provided in e-discovery, informational retrieval tools are the best alternative to expensive fishing expeditions.

The most fundamental advice for attorneys encountering e-discovery is to have a firm understanding of your obligations under the federal rules and the rules that are applicable to your jurisdiction, because the consequences of not complying with those rules can be drastic.

Key Takeaways

- As an attorney in this practice area, you need to examine your client's current document and data retention policy, and determine what efficiencies presently exist. A thorough understanding of the client's data management system is crucial to understanding what information has been preserved and how it is stored. Ultimately, you need to identify the documents that are relevant, and determine how those documents will be collected, processed, reviewed, and produced.
- Clients and attorneys who do not disclose e-discovery information could face sanctions ranging from monetary fines and adverse inference instructions to dismissal of claims and defenses. Consequently, each client and attorney should utilize and develop best practices to ensure that the client and attorney are complying with the e-discovery rules.
- Throughout litigation, you need to work with your client to ensure that effective e-discovery strategies and policies are followed; initiating a litigation hold when the party reasonably anticipated litigation, maintaining the litigation hold, documenting the methodologies used in culling the ESI, and carefully reviewing the data to prevent inadvertent disclosure of privileged information are the keys to successfully navigating the e-discovery process.
- The most fundamental advice for an attorney in this practice area is to have a firm understanding of your obligations under the federal rules and the rules that are applicable to your jurisdiction, because the consequences of not complying with those rules can be drastic.

Christopher G. Buenik, a partner at Bollinger, Ruberry & Garvey, specializes in all aspects of complex litigation matters with an emphasis in construction litigation and defense of industrial, commercial, and residential clients involving OSHA citations, contract disputes, insurance coverage, business disruption, mechanics liens, personal injury, and property damage claims. He also provides representation in insurance defense, general tort, subrogation, transportation, product defect, and premises liability matters.

Mr. Buenik is a member of the Chicago Bar Association and Defense Research Institute. He was recognized by Illinois Super Lawyers *(2008-2010) as a Rising Star in Construction Litigation. Mr. Buenik is admitted to practice before the Supreme Court of Illinois (2001) and the U.S. District Court for the Northern District of Illinois (2001).*

Mr. Buenik received his B.A. in political science from the University of Wisconsin-Madison in 1994 and his J.D., cum laude, from The John Marshall Law School in 2001 where he was marketing editor of The John Marshall Journal of Computer and Information Law. *He was a team member in both the Wagner National Labor & Employment Law Moot Court Competition and ABA Regional Negotiation Competition.*

APPENDICES

APPENDIX A

D&G CLIENT PRESERVATION LETTER AND MEMO

[DATE]

Client Contact
Client
Client Address

Re: Document Retention Obligations in Connection with **[Litigation/Subpoena Title]** or **[Pending or Threatened Government Investigation]**

Dear ________:

We are writing in connection with our representation of the Company ("you," "your" or the "Company") in the **[litigation/subpoena with (name of adversary)] or [threatened or pending investigation by (name of Government Agency)]** to advise you of the obligations of the Company and its employees concerning the retention of documents relevant to the **[litigation/subpoena] or [investigation]**.

As you may be aware, as a result of this **[litigation/subpoena] or [investigation]**, the Company and its employees have a duty to preserve all information that is relevant to the issues that have been or may be raised in the **[litigation/subpoena] or [investigation]**. **[For investigation – These obligations arise from such laws as the Sarbanes Oxley Act.]** These obligations include preserving not only hard copies of all relevant documents, but also all electronic data that the Company and/or employees have concerning these issues, including emails and information stored on network servers, back-up tapes, computer discs, hard drives on office desktops or laptops, hard drives on employees' home desktops or laptops used for Company purposes, PDAs and blackberries. The failure to adhere to these obligations could result in **[for litigation/subpoena - sanctions] or [for investigation - criminal penalties]** against the Company and/or its employees.

The Company and its employees, therefore, are required to save all information, electronic or otherwise, that is relevant to the pending **[litigation/subpoena] or [investigation]**. This includes all documents in paper and electronic form. Electronic documents include information from network servers, back-up tapes, other electronic storage, computer discs, hard drives on office desktops or laptops, hard drives on employees' home desktops or laptops used for Company purposes, PDAs, blackberries, and any other source that contains information relevant to the pending **[litigation/subpoena] or [investigation]**.

In accordance with these obligations, the Company must immediately send out the attached preservation memorandum to its IT personnel and all employees that may possess relevant information. **[If known - Based upon the information available to us at this time, we believe the following employees may have relevant information concerning the [litigation/subpoena] or [investigation] and thus, should be sent the attached preservation letter: [list employees]. This list may not include all employees with potentially relevant information and you should check your records to determine whether other employees may have relevant information concerning the [litigation/subpoena] or [investigation].]** We ask that the Company also keep a record of who was sent the attached preservation memo. If at a later date we or the Company determine that additional employees may have relevant information concerning the **[litigation/subpoena] or [investigation]**, you should also send to these individuals the preservation memo.

We will also need to speak to the person(s) at the Company firm in charge of electronic data storage. Please provide us with their contact information so that we may go over with them the steps that need to be taken to preserve all forms of electronic data in connection with the **[litigation/subpoena] or [investigation]**.

If you have any questions, please do not hesitate to contact us.

Sincerely yours,

[your name]

PRIVILEGED AND CONFIDENTIAL ATTORNEY WORK PRODUCT AND/OR ATTORNEY-CLIENT COMMUNICATION

MEMORANDUM

To:	Employee	**Date:**	
From:	General Counsel/IT Department/or Other	**File No:**	
CC:	IT Department/General Counsel		
Re:	Preservation of Electronic Documents and Other Information		

This memorandum is to inform you that the Company [is or may become] involved in [a litigation with (name of adversary)/subpoena] or [is aware that it is being investigated by a (name of Federal Agency)]. As you may be aware, as a result of this [claim/litigation/subpoena] or [investigation], you and the Company have a duty to preserve all information that is relevant to the issues that may be raised in the [litigation] or [investigation]. This obligation includes preserving not only hard copies of all relevant documents, but also any electronic data you may have concerning these issues, including emails and information stored on network servers, back-up tapes, computer discs, office desktops or laptops, employees' home desktops or laptops used for Company purposes, PDAs and blackberries. The failure to adhere to these obligations could result in [for litigation/subpoena - sanctions] or [for investigation – fines and/or criminal penalties] against you and/or the Company .

As such, you are now required to save all information, electronic or otherwise, that is relevant to the pending **[claim/litigation/subpoena] or [investigation]**. This includes saving information on network servers, back-up tapes, computer discs, office desktops or laptops, home desktops or laptops used for Company purposes, PDAs and blackberries and any other source that contains information relevant to the pending **[claim/litigation/subpoena] or [investigation]**.

Your receipt of this memorandum is solely because the Company has determined that you may possess information relevant to the pending **[claim/litigation/subpoena] or [investigation]** and does not necessarily mean that you will be involved in the **[claim/litigation/subpoena] or [investigation]**. If you have any questions regarding these obligations, please feel free to contact **[name of the individual in charge of document retention for the claim/litigation/subpoena or investigation]**.

Courtesy of Michael C. Lasky and Marc J. Rachman, Davis & Gilbert LLP

APPENDIX B

PRESERVATION CHECKLIST

ELECTRONIC DISCOVERY BEST PRACTICES
Preservation Checklist

When to commence preservation efforts:

Preservation efforts should be commenced at the earliest opportunity after any of the following events:

- Service of a Complaint (if the client is a defendant)
- Service of a subpoena
- Service of a request for documents
- A party reasonably anticipates litigating a claim
- Receipt of notice of a threatened or pending government investigation

Who to contact:

If you do not already have a contact at the client, identify who your contact(s) should be. Often the Chief Financial Officer or another senior-level executive will be your first point of contact. He or she may want to delegate responsibility for document preservation to someone else, particularly if he or she was not directly involved in the matter at issue. Your contact should be a senior-level employee who either has knowledge about the matters at issue in the litigation or investigation or can help you get in touch with those employees who do.

What to do:

✓ Send a letter to your client contact describing preservation duties, and enclosing a memo that can be distributed to all employees with potentially relevant information, including employee(s) who will supervise document preservation efforts and IT personnel.

- ✓ Identify senior-level employee(s) responsible for supervising document preservation efforts and senior-level employee(s) in the IT department with an understanding of the client's ESI retention policies and procedures.

- ✓ Identify all other employees who may have potentially relevant information.

- ✓ Confirm that the preservation memo has been circulated to IT and Records departments, as well as to all other employees with potentially relevant information.

- ✓ Schedule discussions with IT, employee(s) responsible for supervising document preservation efforts, and any employee(s) with potentially relevant documents or their supervisor.

Questions to ask:

(1) These questions can be used to guide discussions with clients in order to make informed decisions and recommendations.

Questions for IT:

Document Retention Protocols:

- Do you have a written document retention protocol for electronic documents?
  - If so, ask for a copy and review it.
    - Ask if they always follow the written protocol or if their practice deviates from it.
    - Recommend any changes necessary to protocols to ensure that potentially relevant documents are not deleted.
  - If not, ask about practices and unwritten protocols concerning retention/deletion of e-mails and other electronic documents.
    - Do you back up e-mails?
    - Do you back up other electronic documents?

        - On employees' local computer drives?
        - On any shared drive?
        - On any other file server?
    - How often are back-up copies made?
    - Where are back-up copies kept?
    - How long are back-up copies kept?
    - What is the oldest back-up tape or other back-up copy that you still have?

Understanding the Relevant Systems:

- What kind of computers do employees use?
    - Macs
    - PCs
    - Desktop computers
    - Laptops

E-mail System:

- What e-mail system do you use?
    - Microsoft Outlook
    - Lotus Notes
    - Other
- Has the e-mail system changed in the past (1 year/3 years/5 years or any other relevant period)?
    - When did it change?
    - What happened to employees' e-mails that were on the server at the time of the change?
        - Were they migrated to a new program?
        - Were they deleted?
        - Were they archived and retained?
            - Are there any restrictions on employees' ability to retain e-mails?
    - Date restrictions
        - *E.g.*, are all e-mails older than 180 days automatically deleted?
    - Size restrictions

        - *E.g.*, are employees allowed to keep only 500 MB of e-mails at any given time?
- Are these universal restrictions or do different restrictions apply to different groups of employees?
    - *E.g.*, are senior executives allowed unlimited e-mail storage, while junior-level staff are restricted?
- Can employees archive e-mails locally to their computers?
- Are e-mails of former employees ever retained?
    - Under what circumstances
    - Where are they retained?
    - How long are they retained?

Other Electronic Documents:

- Do employees save documents they are working on locally to their computer hard drives?
- Do employees save documents they access or work on to a shared drive?
    - How is the shared drive organized?
    - Is the shared drive searchable?
    - Are there any automatic deletion processes that affect documents on the shared drive?
- Do employees work at home?
    - If so, do they log on to the client's server?
    - Can they access company e-mails from home?
    - Does the company provide employees with laptops or desktop computers to use at home?
- Do employees input information into any special or proprietary programs?
    - *E.g.*, timekeeping programs, payroll programs, accounting programs, sales tracking programs, etc.
- Do employees use instant messaging or other electronic methods of communication (such as Facebook or LinkedIn) in their work?
    - If so, are records of these communications maintained?
    - If so, how, where and for how long?
- What are your in-house search capabilities?

    - If I wanted to get all e-mails sent to or from John Doe between January 1 and June 1, 2010, are you able to search and collect only those e-mails?
    - If I wanted to get all e-mails referring to Product X, can you run keyword searches across all employees' e-mails on your server?

Questions for Records:

If the client has a records department separate and apart from its IT, questions should include:

- Is there a document retention protocol for storage of hard copy documents?
    - If so, ask for a copy and review it.
    - If not, ask about practices and unwritten rules regarding retention of paper documents.
- Does the company have any offsite paper record storage?
    - If so, what is kept there?
    - How is it organized?
    - How long are records kept offsite?
- Does the company have any records storage facilities on the premises?
    - If so, what is stored there?
    - How is it organized?
    - How long are records kept there?
        - Note that many clients do not have centralized record-keeping facilities on or offsite, but may have file cabinets or other document storage facilities assigned to particular departments or employees.

Questions for individual employees:

Background information:

- Did you do any work that may be relevant to the case/investigation?
- What work did you do?

  - Did anyone else do that work?
  - Who?
- What was your title?
  - Has that changed over time?
- Who did you report to?
  - Has that changed over time?
- How long have you been with the company?
- How long were you working on the [potentially relevant project/assignment/client/issue]?
- What were your duties and responsibilities for the [potentially relevant project/assignment/client/issue]?

Communications:

- Who did you communicate with, generally, concerning this work?
  - Which co-workers did you communicate with?
    - Which of them are still with the company?
    - If any have left – when did they leave?
  - Did you communicate with any outside vendors, client contacts, etc?
  - Who?
- Did you communicate by e-mails, instant messages, telephone or any other methods?
  - Did you keep copies of these communications or any notes about these communications?
  - Where are these documents now?
- How far back do your e-mails go?
  - Are you a "keeper" or a "deleter"?
  - Do you file your e-mails in relevant subfolders?
- When you work on a document concerning the [potentially relevant project/assignment/client/issue], where do you save it?
- Do you delete these documents?
- Do you still have these documents?
- Are they in any particular file or folder on your computer or the company server?

Hard copy files:

Hard copy files should be copied and the location of original documents should be recorded.

- Do you tend to keep hard copy files concerning the work you do?
- Do you still have any hard copy files concerning the [potentially relevant project/assignment/client/issue]?
  - Where are they now?
  - What do you have?
  - Did you send any of your files concerning the [potentially relevant project/assignment/client/issue] to offsite storage?
  - When?

What to do next:

- Record dates of receipt and distribution of the preservation memo to employees.
- Take steps to reduce the risks associated with accidental loss of data.
  - Consider copying documents to a secure location and/or imaging hard drives.
    - Investigate the costs/practicalities of copying documents to a secure location or imaging the hard drives of all employees with potentially relevant information.
  - In many cases e-mails currently on a server or archived on a user's local drives should be copied to avoid the risk of loss through end-user error at a later time.
    - If not impractical, e-mails of key employees currently on the client's server should be copied to external drives or DVDs.
    - If not impractical, e-mails archived locally on a user's computer should be copied to external drives or DVDs.

    - If the volume of e-mails renders copying users' entire collection impractical, keyword searches sufficiently broad to capture all potentially responsive documents may be used to collect an appropriate subset of e-mails for preservation.
  - Other electronic documents should also be copied and preserved.
    - Depending on the needs of a particular case, it may be possible to copy electronic documents from shared network drives and local drives to DVDs or external drives for preservation purposes.
    - In some instances an exact image of the document rather than a copy will be necessary.
      - Imaging hard drives is the best way to ensure going forward that no electronic data is destroyed. Once an employee's hard drive is imaged, there is a preserved record of everything that was on that employee's computer at the time of the imaging.
  - Consider restoration of deleted files.
    - Rarely does a Client's IT department know the proper methods to restore deleted files without actually destroying potentially relevant information. It is not worth the risk of losing potentially relevant data to have the Client restore deleted files from a hard drive. Have restoration of deleted files done by an outside vendor.
    - This is different than the restoration of files from back-up tapes, which can be done by the Client if the Client has the necessary resources.
- Follow up with the client and send periodic reminders concerning the obligation to preserve potentially relevant information.
- Promptly inform the client of any change in the scope of documents that must be preserved.

- Ask the client to let you know if any employees previously identified as possessing potentially relevant information are terminated or leave.
    - Before any departing employees' desktop or laptop computers are recycled, discarded, wiped clean or given to other employees to use:
        - Ensure that all potentially relevant information has been copied or imaged.
        - In some cases, it may be necessary to image the entire hard drive.
        - As an alternative, the hard drive may be quarantined, but this may be costlier in the long run than imaging.
    - Collect all potentially relevant information and documents from the employee's hard copy files.

Chain of Custody:

Maintain a written record of the chain of custody of all copies of electronic documents made by client.

- For copies of electronic files burned to disc from a hard drive and hard drive images, make sure there is a record of the date the disk was burned or the image was made, who burned the disc or made the image and from what computer the files were copied or imaged.
- For copies of electronic files burned to disc from a backup tape, make sure there is a record of the description of the back-up tape (e.g., the date the back-up tape was made, what was contained on the back-up tape and the volume name of the back-up tape), who restored the data from the back-up tape and when and who burned the restored data from the back-up tape to disk and when.

Courtesy of Michael C. Lasky & Marc J. Rachman, Davis & Gilbert LLP

APPENDIX C

WHEN DOES IT END?

When does the duty to preserve end?

The duty to preserve electronically stored information (ESI) potentially relevant to litigation and the penalties for failing to properly and timely comply with this duty are well-documented. We have all heard the horror stories, read the ever-evolving body of cases, and been bombarded by cautionary White Papers from vendors and service providers. Parties in both state and federal courts frequently argue about when the duty to preserve attaches in a particular case, and Judges regularly sanction parties who fail to take reasonable steps to preserve relevant information after the duty arises.

But one important question is not often addressed by the courts or commentators: "When does the duty to preserve end?" The answer to this question is significant for a number of reasons which relate to the larger issues associated with defensible, cost-effective practices regarding the management, collection, review, and production of ESI.

Why does it matter?

Prematurely releasing a litigation hold and allowing potentially relevant ESI to be lost or destroyed can lead to sanctions in the same manner as failing to properly implement the hold in the first place. On the other hand, failing to timely release a litigation hold can increase the burdens and costs associated with managing the massive amount of ESI generated every day by businesses of all sizes.

The burdens and costs associated with maintaining ESI, including ESI that was taken out of the normal data management and destruction lifecycle for a litigation hold, can, and often do, far outweigh the cost savings and risk aversion that comes with following a defensible, consistent process for managing ESI. Recognition of the risks and costs associated with maintaining ESI beyond is useful life is inspiring many companies that have not already done so to create or revise data management policies and litigation readiness plans. If implemented and followed consistently, such plans can significantly reduce the costs and risks associated with amassing stock-piles of emails, Power Point Presentations, and company retreat photos. Any effective data management or litigation readiness policy should include defensible procedures for releasing ESI from a litigation hold.

Why is this a difficult question?

The timing of when to release ESI from a litigation hold may seem as simple as "when the case ends." Unfortunately, many situations which trigger a preservation obligation do not have an easily identifiable trigger for its release. For example, even a lawsuit that results in a settlement may not trigger a release if there are other similarly situated plaintiffs who are likely to file suit. No existing rule or case law provides a convenient check-list for when the duty to preserve ESI expires, and courts will likely assess these issues on a case-specific basis using the same fact-specific inquiry they use to assess when the preservation obligation is triggered.

Courts have held that the obligation to preserve evidence is triggered "when the party has notice that the evidence is relevant to litigation or when a party should have known that the evidence may be relevant to future litigation." Cache La Poudre Feeds, LLC v. Land O'Lakes, Inc., 244 F.R.D. 614, 620 (D. Colo. 2007) (quoting Zublake v. UBS Warburg, LLC, 220 F.R.D. 212, 216 (S.D.N.Y. 2003)). Recognizing that "litigation is an ever-present possibility in our society," the duty to preserve requires that future litigation is not merely possible, but probable. UMG Recordings, Inc. v. Hummer Winblad Venture Partners, 462 F. Supp. 2d 1060, 1068 (N.D. Cal. 2006); Cache La Poudre Feeds, 244 F.R.D. at 621.

As illustrated by the case law in this area, determining when future litigation goes from possible to probable is a fact-specific inquiry that illustrates the difficulty in knowing when the duty to preserve has ended. A few examples and the dilemmas they create include:

- Company A receives a preservation notice and a clear threat of future patent infringement litigation. Assuming the letter is sufficient to trigger the duty to preserve, how long does the obligation last? What if the lawsuit isn't filed for a year, or two, or three, or ten? Does the trigger ever expire?

- What if the patent infringement lawsuit is actually filed against Company A along with several other similar companies, but then Company A gets dismissed from the lawsuit without prejudice? Does the resolution of the underlying case end Company A's preservation obligation or is Complaint A required to continue to preserve and wait to see if the claimant decides to refile?
- What if Company A never receives any preservation notice, is not sued, but is in a similar position to other companies who are sued? Should Company A anticipate that future litigation is probable?

The patent infringement aspect of the hypothetical examples above adds the complicating factor of a relatively long statute of limitations period which makes the option of triggering a release based on the date when the statue of limitations expires less viable. Unfortunately, companies will have to take a case-specific approach, guided by established protocols and guidelines, to determine when a particular hold can be released. Absent a clear directive from the courts on when a duty to preserve expires, the best guidance comes from the cases addressing when the hold is triggered.

For example, UMG Recordings, Inc. v. Hummer Winblad Venture Partners, 462 F. Supp. 2d 1060 (N.D. Cal. 2006) illustrates the risks associated with failing to issue and maintain a litigation hold during a series of related lawsuits, including after a company has been dismissed from a lawsuit. The UMG Recordings, Inc. case is one of a series of related lawsuits involving claims of copyright infringement against Napster brought by recording industry plaintiffs. Hummer Winblad Venture Partners ("Hummer") became an investor in Napster in May 2000 - when Napster was involved in several pending lawsuits (collectively the "Napster I litigation"). One month later, on June 1, 2000, Hummer was served with deposition and document subpoenas requesting communications related to Napster in the Napster I litigation. Two days after receiving the subpoenas, a Hummer executive sent an email out to all Hummer employees which the court later found instructed employees to delete all Napster-related emails going forward in order to avoid producing them ("June 3, 2000 Email"). Later that same month, an officer of Hummer was advised by the CEO of

Universal Music Corporation that the recording companies intended to sue Napster's investment firms if the alleged copyright infringement continued. In July of 2000, a lawsuit was filed against Napster and other defendants, including Hummer ("Katz lawsuit").

The Katz lawsuit was subsequently dismissed in July of 2001, but the Napster I litigation remained ongoing. In August of 2001, as part of the settlement negotiations in Napster I, counsel for plaintiffs sent Hummer a letter threatening litigation. Hummer acknowledged that it knew it was going to be sued in an April 2002 email sent to a potential purchaser of Hummer, and one year later, in April of 2003, the instant lawsuit was filed.

When Hummer produced the June 3, 2000 email as part of the UMG Recording, Inc. litigation, the plaintiffs sought sanctions against Hummer for failing to preserve relevant ESI. The court had to determine not only when the duty to preserve was triggered, but whether, as Hummer argued, Hummer's preservation obligation ended after the Katz lawsuit was dismissed. Hummer argued that the dismissal of the Katz case in July of 2001, to which it was a named party, terminated any preservation obligation and no new obligation to preserve was triggered until Hummer was served with the UMG Recordings, Inc. complaint in August of 2003. The plaintiffs argued that the preservation obligation was triggered in May of 2000, when Hummer invested in Napster, and remained in effect through the current litigation.

The court held that the initial preservation trigger occurred in June of 2000 when the CEO of Universal Music told an executive at Hummer that it planned to sue the company. The court held that this clear statement of intent to sue coupled with the existing related litigation was sufficient to trigger a preservation obligation. The court also held that Hummer's duty to preserve was not released upon dismissal of the Katz lawsuit because Hummer was aware "there was a reasonable probability of litigation against Hummer during the period following the Katz lawsuit." Notably, the court held that Hummer's status as an investor in Napster and Hummer's receipt of a third-party subpoena in the Napster I litigation were ***not*** enough alone to create a reasonable expectation that litigation against Hummer was probable rather than just possible.

The additional surrounding circumstances that elevated the threat of litigation against Hummer from possible to probable included 1) Hummer's receipt of a letter treating suit in August 2001, one month after the Katz litigation was dismissed; 2) John Hummer's admission to a potential purchaser in April 2002 that he knew Hummer would be sued; 3) Hummer's past status as a party in the Katz lawsuit; and 4) Napster's bankruptcy and the plaintiffs litigation strategy to pursue solvent investors.

Accordingly, the court found that Hummer had at worst "mounted a knowing and concerted effort to destroy Napster-related emails that it had a duty to preserve and produce" and at best had best "grossly negligent in executing its duties to preserve evidence. . . ." The court concluded that an adverse inference instruction and monetary sanctions were warranted.

The court's fact-specific holding does not provide a clear test for when a preservation obligation expires, but it does offer some additional factors to consider when assessing when to release legal holds, including

- Whether similarly situated parties have been sued in other litigation;
- Whether the company has been involved in similar litigation in the past; and
- Whether plaintiffs or potential plaintiffs have communicated an intention to sue (or refile).

Companies balancing the costs and burdens of preservation against the risks associated with failing to preserve potentially relevant information must carefully weigh the risks and burdens and evaluate the specific circumstances that triggered the hold in the first instance. Companies may want to consider adding certain factors or timelines into their own policies that show a good faith and consistent approach to making these determinations.

The general guiding theme in determining when a litigation hold can be released is the same as whether it has been triggered: does litigation continue to be probable rather than merely possible? The fact-specific answer to that question requires careful assessment of the particular circumstances of the case in light of the company's established practices and procedures for management of ESI. A consistent approach that considers such factors as those identified in the UMG Recordings, Inc. opinion reduces the costs and burden associated with keeping the preserved ESI out of the regular data management lifecycle while providing a defensible process in the event the timing of the release of a litigation hold is ever called into question.

Courtesy of Alison A. Grounds, Troutman Sanders LLP

APPENDIX D

THE *ZUBULAKE* FACTORS

- Institute a litigation hold to strategically retain, preserve, and access electronic documents and data during litigation.

- Periodically reissue the litigation hold to ensure compliance by new and continuing employees.

- Monitor the litigation's important players compliance with the litigation hold.

- Direct client employees to search for, retain, and provide electronic documents and data for production.

- Coordinate with IT department to ensure safe storage of electronic data.

Courtesy of Christopher G. Buenik, Bollinger, Ruberry & Garvey

APPENDIX E

E-DISCOVERY CHECKLIST

- Familiarize yourself with client operations, including information systems.
- Determine types of information maintained (data categories).
- Map the network architecture.
- Determine how information flows through the network.
- Determine procedures for retrieval.
- Determine costs of retrieval.
- Determine costs of past restoration attempts.
- Determine and document "routine good-faith operation of your electronic information system."
- Review document & data retention policy.
- Determine deficiencies in policy and remedy.
- Disseminate document and data retention policy to key personnel.
- Educate clients and employees of the client that the duty to preserve starts when they "reasonably anticipated litigation."
- Implement litigation hold procedures and notices.
- Review and update litigation hold notice.
- Educate and train employees of the client to understand the policy and purpose of the document & data retention policy.
- Interview document custodians.
- Send follow up litigation hold notices.
- Monitor litigation hold efforts on a recurring basis.
- Seek preservation order or send preservation letter.
- Determine best methods for collection.
- Document collection and chain-of-custody.
- Confer with opposing counsel to identify the electronic discovery issues and agree on a plan.
- Confer with opposing counsel regarding clawback or quick peek agreements.
- Confer with opposing counsel regarding key word searches.

- Confer with opposing counsel regarding beginning and ending dates for document & data collection.
- Confer with opposing counsel regarding key witnesses.
- Determine form of production.
- Determine need for cost-shifting.
- Determine how to deal with duplicates.
- Determine need for redaction.
- Formulate discovery plan.
- Address electronic discovery issues early on with initial disclosures. Fed. R. Civ. P. 26(a)(1).
- Document electronic discovery plan, including issues, employees consulted and conclusions reached.
- Review the client's formalized backup protocol.
- Determine financial and resource burden to suspend the customary practice of rotating or recycling backup tapes, tape storage costs, and other expenses.
- Determine the physical location of the backup tapes, i.e. off-site or on-site.
- Segregate and secure backup tapes subject to litigation hold.

Identify Key Information Technology (IT) Personnel

- Establish relationship with pertinent IT personnel.
- Designate and prepare IT personnel to act as 30(b)(6) witness.
- Provide guidance to IT personnel about document & data retention plan, destruction and enforcement of the document & data retention policy.
- Educate IT personnel regarding types of information normally requested through discovery process.
- Educate IT personnel on life cycle of a litigation matter and where help will be necessary.
- Request IT personnel to keep an inventory of stored information.
- Request IT personnel to organize data storage efforts and establish systems that simplify the later identification, retrieval, and production of information.

- Inform IT personnel of the need to document all installations, changes, modifications, upgrades and patches of all hardware and software.
- Review the document request with IT personnel; do not assume that requests are self-explanatory.

E-Discovery Checklist, *available at* http://www.iediscovery.com/files/resources/E-discovery_Checklist_0307.pdf (Last visited June 22, 2010).

Courtesy of Christopher G. Buenik, Bollinger, Ruberry & Garvey